WITHDRAWN

Speech and Hearing Problems

Frontispiece: You can help him learn to talk.

SPEECH AND
HEARING PROBLEMS

A Guide for Teachers and Parents

By

CHARLES E. PALMER, Ph.D.

Assistant Professor
Speech and Hearing Consultant
Special Education Center
Northwestern State College
Natchitoches, Louisiana

With a Foreword by

JOHN W. KIDD, Ed.D.

Director, Special Education Center
Northwestern State College
Natchitoches, Louisiana

CHARLES C THOMAS · PUBLISHER
Springfield · Illinois · U.S.A.

CHARLES C THOMAS • PUBLISHER

BANNERSTONE HOUSE

301-327 East Lawrence Avenue, Springfield, Illinois, U.S.A.

© *1961 by* CHARLES C THOMAS • PUBLISHER

Library of Congress Catalog Card Number: 61-10379

With THOMAS BOOKS careful attention is given to all details of manufacturing and design. It is the Publisher's desire to present books that are satisfactory as to their physical qualities and artistic possibilities and appropriate for their particular use. THOMAS BOOKS will be true to those laws of quality that assure a good name and good will.

Printed in the United States of America

To my students . . . .
past, present, and future

foreword

AFTER A QUARTER-CENTURY of professional work with exceptional children, particularly with children having speech and/or hearing disorders, Charles E. Palmer has both the theoretical understanding and the practical "know-how" to render the advice enclosed between these covers. Further, he has been able to hew to the line of fine distinction of what may be delegated to the parent and/or teacher in working with speech and hearing problems and that which is, of necessity, reserved as properly among the prerogatives of his profession.

I suspect that Dr. Palmer's experience in public speaking has been of significant assistance as revealed by the chatty, informal, well-illustrated, easy-to-read style he uses to present professionally reliable information.

He has earned the B.A., B.D., M.A., and Ph.D. degrees, and holds Advanced Certification in Speech Pathology from the American Speech and Hearing Association. He has been a classroom teacher, a speech correctionist, a teacher of speech-reading, and the supervisor of a county program of services for handicapped children. In his present position as Speech and Hearing Consultant, he teaches courses that deal with speech and hearing problems, evaluates the speech and hearing problems of school children, and confers with teachers and parents.

In preparing this book he has undoubtedly performed a real service to those who are concerned with speech and/or hearing problems.

JOHN W. KIDD, ED.D.
Director, Special Education Center
Northwestern State College
Natchitoches, Louisiana

PREFACE

A LETTER TO PARENTS AND TEACHERS

Dear Reader:

Some parents and teachers are unduly concerned about the speech and hearing of children. Sometimes they suffer needless anguish, and sometimes—in their anxiety—they actually create problems where none had existed.

Others do not seem to be aware of defective speech or impaired hearing, nor of the far-reaching effects such handicaps may have upon a child's educational progress and emotional adjustment.

Still others recognize the problems and are eager to help, but do not know what to do or where to turn for help.

This book has been written to:

answer   some of the questions that parents and teachers frequently ask about speech and hearing problems;

explain what you may do when professional therapists are not available, and to

suggest ways in which you, the parent or teacher, may assist the professional worker if a child is enrolled in a special program for speech and/or hearing problems.

This is a "first aid manual." It is not a substitute for the work of a professionally prepared speech correctionist or teacher of the deaf. In fact, it is probably unwise for a parent or a teacher to initiate a program of correction without first securing professional advice.

If professional help is not available, this book will enable you to "do something"—something helpful and constructive. If professional guidance is available, it will help you to understand the speech correction or hearing rehabilitation program and to cooperate more effectively.

During the pre-school years the parents play an all-important role as the "teachers of speech." Later they will share the responsibility with the classroom teacher and, in some instances, with the speech correctionist. The importance of the role of the parents can hardly be over-emphasized. A number of speech pathologists have said that THE BIGGEST STUMBLING BLOCK TO THE CHILD IN THE ACQUISITION OF SPEECH IS THE TEACHING METHOD USED BY THE PARENTS. That is a serious charge. Let's consider it for a moment.

Would you send your child to a school conducted by "teachers" who had no professional preparation? Not if you could help it! You'd say, "Anything as important as my child's education will be entrusted only to those who have had the best possible education and preferably some sound experience." Yet in this most important period, when a child is facing the complex and confusing problem of learning speech, we blithely assume that we can do the job.

While it is true that most children acquire speech even when the teaching is exceedingly poor, some children require more skillful teaching, and all would profit from it.

Because the teaching method you use with your child is of tremendous importance, because there are things that you can do to make the learning of speech easier for your child (whether he has normal hearing or a severe hearing loss), because there is so much that you can do to help your child become a happy, well-adjusted person in spite of a speech or hearing problem—these are the reasons for the writing of this book.

There is no magic formula to be found in these pages. The improvement of speech involves the breaking down of well-established neuro-muscular patterns and the building up of new patterns. Lip-reading (or speech-reading, as it is often called) is a skill that is not easily acquired. Time and patience are necessary. But with sympathetic, intelligent help, the time can be shortened, frustration and anxiety can be minimized, and most children can be helped to acquire adequate mastery of the important skills needed for communication. This book contains information and suggestions that should help you move toward this goal.

C. E. P.

acknowledgments

SOMEONE HAS SAID, "There is nothing new under the sun." Be that as it may, I am indebted to my teachers, to the authors of books and articles, to lecturers, to the children with whom I have worked, to their parents, to my students, and to my colleagues for many of the ideas presented in this book. It is impossible to name all of those who have contributed in one way or another to the contents of this manuscript, but I have been strongly influenced by Dr. John V. Irwin, Director of the Speech and Hearing Clinics, University of Wisconsin-Madison; Miss Alice H. Streng, Chairman, Department of Exceptional Education, University of Wisconsin-Milwaukee, and Mrs. Gretchen Phair, Supervisor of Speech Correction, Bureau for Handicapped Children, Madison, Wisconsin.

More specifically, appreciation is expressed to:

Dr. John W. Kidd, Director, Special Education Center, Northwestern State College, Natchitoches, Louisiana, for his encouragement and helpful criticism during the preparation of the manuscript,

Mr. Thomas L. Hennigan. Director of Audio-Visual Services, Northwestern State College, for the pictures used as illustrations,

Winifred N. Palmer, my wife, whose name might well appear as co-author,

Beth Armagost, for her suggestions and painstaking editing of the manuscript.

C.E.P.

CONTENTS

Speech and Hearing Problems

PART I

speech
problems

chapter i

some questions and answers about speech problems

Many books have been written about speech problems, but parents and teachers do not always have time to read them. Listed below are some of the questions frequently asked about speech. Brief answers are given to each.

1. Do many children have speech problems?

It is estimated by national authorities that about ten percent of our school children have speech problems. To put it another way, about ten children out of one hundred need help in acquiring acceptable standards of speech. About half of these (five out of one hundred) have speech problems or defects of such severity that it interferes seriously with their school progress and social adjustment.

2. Isn't that a surprisingly large number?

No, not when you consider the complexity of speech. To describe what the brain, nerves, and muscles must do in order to produce the single sound of "p" requires ten to twelve pages in the average sized textbook. We don't expect children to become concert violinists without expert teaching. Yet speech is much more complex than the playing of a violin. The surprising fact is that so many children learn to talk adequately without any help except what the family casually provides.

3. What is a speech defect?

Quite a wide range of speech patterns is considered "normal." It is only when the speech of an individual differs significantly from the speech of others in the same community of the same age and sex that we may say speech is defective.

The two purposes of speech are to satisfy the need for self-expression and to provide meaningful communication. When speech cannot adequately serve these purposes, it is defective.

Not all speech *differences* are speech *defects*. To be called a "speech defect," the "speech difference" must be great enough to call attention to itself or to interfere with communication. Seldom is a young child aware of his speech differences. But when he does become aware of the fact that his speech is different, he may become maladjusted. Some children with defective speech find that it is easier to refuse to talk than to do their best at expressing themselves only to be teased and humiliated. Such withdrawn behavior interferes with progress in school and with social development. Other children react to teasing about their speech by becoming overly aggressive, resentful, antagonistic. Sometimes the maladjustment is the most serious aspect of the speech problem.

4. What are the types of speech disorders?

Articulation is the most common type of speech disorder among children. Disorders of articulation are characterized by the omission, distortion, or substitution of speech sounds. "Tootie" instead of "cookie," "wed" instead of "red," "thop" or "top" instead of "stop"—these are examples of common articulatory errors. Sometimes only one or two sounds are defective, but sometimes there are so many errors that the speech is unintelligible to everyone with the possible exception of the parents.

Voice problems (disorders of phonation) are not as common as articulatory problems. They include voices that are too high or too low in pitch, too loud or not loud enough, voices that are harsh, breathy, nasal or otherwise unpleasant, and voices that are monotonous—that is, lacking in flexibility of expression.

Problems of the understanding and use of words constitute another speech or language disorder. Words, of course, are symbols; they "stand for" or represent something. What the word "cat" means to you depends upon all of the past experiences that you associate with that symbol. A child may know that this small animal likes milk, catches mice, has soft fur, and purrs when it is petted—and still be unable to associate or "connect" the word "cat" with the animal. Children who have difficulty in understanding or using words are sometimes referred to as "aphasoid." Authorities differ in their terminology, but the fact remains that some children have great difficulty in dealing with the symbols of language—that is, with the spoken or written word. It is usually quite difficult to diagnose this disorder in young children; the help of various specialists is needed.

Stuttering is probably the speech disorder that causes parents the most anxiety. Some writers believe that it is this very anxiety that contributes to the child's problem. This disorder is usually thought of in terms of hesitations in the flow of speech, repetitions of sounds, words, or phrases, and facial grimaces or tensions. Although there is much more involved in the problem of stuttering than a description of the symptoms, it is these observable symptoms that cause parents to become concerned.

The classification of speech disorders given above is based on symptoms, without consideration for the cause. Under this system a child with a cleft palate, or other physiological defect, would be said to have an articulation problem, a voice problem, or both, depending upon his own speech needs.

5. When should my child begin to talk?

Usually children begin to talk—to use words meaningfully—between the ages of 12 and 18 months. This question is discussed more fully in the next chapter.

6. What is a "qualified speech correctionist"?

A speech correctionist is a person who has had professional preparation in the areas of speech pathology and therapy. Most of the states have set up minimum educational requirements that include preparation in the fields of child development and child psychology as well as speech and hearing pathology. Many states have adopted as their minimum requirements the standards of the American Speech and Hearing Association.

7. Where would I find a speech correctionist?

In some areas, arrangements for consultation with a qualified speech correctionist may be made through the local school authori-

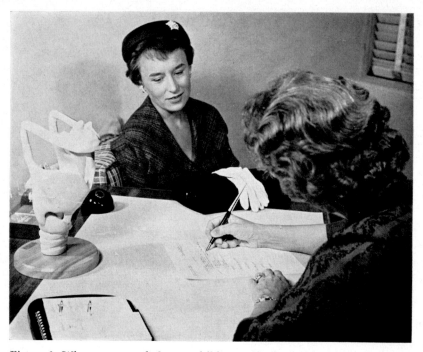

Figure 1: When concerned about a child's speech, do as this mother has done: consult a qualified speech correctionist.

ties. If a speech correctionist is not on the local educational staff, the school authorities and the public health nurse should know what testing or diagnostic and therapeutic services are available. Some state departments of public instruction maintain special education centers that provide diagnostic and consultative services; many colleges have speech and hearing clinics that provide diagnosis (and in some cases therapy) ; and often your own or a neighboring community will have such services available at a center maintained by such an organization as the Crippled Children's Society. You may need to go to the inconvenience of traveling some distance, but you will be glad that you did for one of two reasons: you will learn that the problem is really quite simple, so you can stop worrying about it; or you will find out just how serious the problem is and what should be done about it. In either case, you will be glad that you sought professional advice from a qualified consultant.

A word of caution may be in order. Some excellent speech therapists are in private practice. However, it is possible for an inadequately prepared person to advertise himself as a "speech therapist" or "speech correctionist." Perhaps the best way to check on the qualifications of any person calling himself a speech therapist or correctionist is to write to the American Speech and Hearing Association, 1001 Connecticut Avenue, N. W., Washington 6, D. C. That office will let you know whether or not a person holds basic certification (which means that he meets minimum requirements) or advanced certification (which means that he meets more rigid requirements) in that association, and, at your request, can furnish you with the names of qualified speech therapists in your vicinity.

chapter ii

learning to talk

Parents are frequently concerned about the development of their children. They compare notes. "Jimmy took his first step today!" "Patricia said 'mama' just as plain as could be." "Bobby's not talking yet? Why, when my Sally was only ten months old she . . ."

Sometimes these comparisons cause parents needless anxiety. On the other hand, some parents show an amazing lack of concern even when the neighbors are saying, "I feel sorry for the Browns. There's something wrong with their baby. He's not talking yet, you know."

When should mothers and fathers become concerned about the lack of speech in their children? When should they be concerned about the "baby talk," or the lack of fluency, or the failure to pronounce words correctly?

Before answering these questions, let us briefly review the way in which a child normally acquires speech.

the acquisition of speech

1. What should I watch for?

The acquisition of speech may be traced through some rather definite stages. Of course, they are not mutually exclusive; that is, there will be considerable overlapping, but your enjoyment of your child will be increased if you watch for them.

a. *Reflexive Vocalization.* Upon his arrival in what for him is a foreign land with a foreign language, the newborn infant adds his voice to the babble of unknown tongues. But he has more than a language to learn, for he doesn't even know himself. He must discover his hands and feet and how they may be used. Unacquainted with himself or his environment, the baby responds to any stimulus with all of the resources at his command. This type of response has been called "total and undifferentiated." A pain in his tummy, a pin prick, a loud noise—all cause him to cry and wiggle and thrash

10

about with arms and legs. Crying at this stage is simply the result of air being reflexively expelled by the lungs and passing over the vocal folds that are tense enough to vibrate and produce sound. But even though these sounds are produced without conscious purpose and have no specific meaning, they are the baby's response to stimuli.

Before the second or third week has passed, a careful observer begins to notice differences in the baby's responses. His cry doesn't always sound the same. He is already beginning to differentiate between various kinds of discomfort and other stimuli, and the variety in his crying indicates that he is beginning to recognize these differences. For example, he cries when he is hungry, as he did earlier, but there is a distinct or characteristic sound. Mothers soon learn to recognize the "hunger cry" of an infant.

During these first weeks the non-crying sounds that he makes will be relatively few. In them you'll hear the consonant sounds of *k, l,* and *g,* and most of the vowel sounds that are made at the front of the mouth—including *e* (as in k*e*ep), *i* (as in *i*t) and *a* (as in th*a*t).

Although he is still not aware of his growing repertoire of vocalizations, he soon learns that crying makes a difference! If he cries long enough and loudly enough, something is done about the disagreeable situation. Perhaps this is the beginning of his awareness of the importance of vocal communication!

At any rate, he is acquiring one of the skills needed for speech, for in crying he practices the short, quick inhalation and the prolonged exhalation which he will later use in a more meaningful—and more socially acceptable—mode of communication.

b. *Babbling.* When the baby is about seven weeks old he begins to show that he is aware of the sounds that he makes. Furthermore, he enjoys making them.

And such variety! With a little imagination you can hear Greek, Chinese, and Arabic in his babbling. The fact is, babies of all nationalities make the same sounds at this age. These sounds are the result of random activity. Air passes from the lungs over the vocal folds, producing the laryngeal tone; this basic sound is shaped into every voiced sound in the English language—or any other language—by the activity of the jaw, lips, tongue, and palate. The sounds are made by random movements of these articulators, and seldom is the same sound uttered twice in succession.

Even at this age his "speech" is interesting. Of course his repertoire of sounds is quite different from that of adults, but you'll enjoy observing that (1) he uses a greater variety of sounds in his non-crying vocalizations than in crying; (2) he uses more nasal sounds in his crying than he does in his non-crying or contented sounds; and (3) most of the consonant sounds that he produces are those made with the lips (such as the *p* and *b,* and a little later the *m* sound.)

This babbling or vocal play is important to the child's development of speech, for it affords practice in articulation—in using his tongue, lips, jaw, and palate for the production of sounds. Later some of these sounds will be used in true speech.

c. *Lalling.* The third stage of speech development usually begins during the seventh to ninth month and is called "lalling." This stage is characterized by the repetition of heard sounds. Perhaps the great significance of the appearance of this activity is that it indicates that the child is beginning to associate hearing and sound production—an association that is essential for the normal acquisition of speech.

But don't expect him to imitate you. Not yet. He is now learning to imitate himself—and that's quite an achievement! He seems to find great pleasure in the almost endless repetition of such sounds or combinations of sounds as "ba-ba-ba" and "gub-gub-gub." If an occasional repetition of "ma-ma" is heard, don't become too elated. The chances are all against his using these syllables to designate you. But the time will come. Just be patient.

The successful imitation of a sound stimulates him to try again, and this repetition serves as further stimulus. Sometimes a single combination may be practiced for hours—even for days at a time. Listen to him when he's not aware of your presence. He may start out whispering the sound, repeating it, and after a moment, trying it again and again with increasing volume. Then, after a moment, he may repeat the process—this time with increasing variety of pitch and inflection—obviously pleased with the result and with himself.

By this time other interesting developments are taking place. He's making practical use of his repertoire of sounds. This is not yet true speech, but it might be called "socialized vocalization." He uses one cry to attract attention; he makes a particular kind of sound to accompany the physical activity with which he rejects what is offered; and another kind of sound to accompany the muscular responses with which he tries to make his demands known. You'll probably notice that he uses many nasal sounds to express displeasure or rejection, but uses few nasal sounds when he is happy and contented.

Yes, he's beginning to express himself, and he may be quite insistent about it. Now he has become aware of his vocalization as a practical tool—a way of getting what he wants and rejecting what he does not want. And when this happens he has taken a significant step toward the acquisition of true speech.

During this time he has practiced inflections so that questions and demands are differentiated, and he has also practiced some of the back vowels, such as *oo* (p*oo*l), *u* (p*u*t), and probably *aw* (*aw*e). When he has mastered the sound of *o* (as in *o*we) there is cause for rejoicing!

Another interesting—and welcome—development is that he's crying less and spending more time in lalling and babbling, for there is considerable overlapping of these activities. He also shows more comprehension of the gestures you make.

Probably if you interrupt his repetition of "da-da-da" by saying "da-da" he will either eye you with disdain or reply gleefully, "gub-gub." Soon, however, he will be more apt to answer your "da-da" with his own imitation—but that belongs in the next stage of development.

d. *Echolalia*. The preceding stage was characterized by the repetition of sounds which he had heard himself make. But about the ninth or tenth month he will probably begin imitating or echoing sounds made by others. This type of repetition is called "echolalia." But let's not worry about the name. We'll just be glad that now when we say "da-da" our young prince is more likely to delight us with saying "da-da" than dismiss us with "gub-gub."

At first he will imitate only the sounds that he has already practiced during the lalling stage, but soon he will be ready to imitate sounds presented to him—ready, but not always willing. He seems to reserve the right to decide for himself when he will delight us with his imitations. So don't be surprised if, when Aunt Jane arrives, and you tell her how the young genius said "ma-ma" right after you, and just to prove it you try to get him to do it again —don't be surprised if you are met with icy stares or an outburst of "ge-ka-eh-eh-dee-dah!"

After Aunt Jane leaves, you may find that he will not only echo "ma-ma" but will repeat after you sound combinations that are much more complex. Any echoing of the sounds you produce is a marked advance over lalling, for it shows an acoustic awareness of your presence—an awareness of you as a source of sound and sound stimulation.

At this stage he accompanies his gestures with more vocalization than he did earlier, and he seems to discriminate between the tones of anger and praise. Occasionally he may respond with an attempt at speech. But even though he "echoes" words after us, they have no meaning for him. He is simply enjoying the repetition of the sound. He will, however, show increasing interest in isolated words if they are always associated with things that are important to him and to his needs.

This association of certain sounds or words with objects and activities is important for the acquisition of speech, and proceeds according to a process that psychologists call "conditioning." Briefly, it works like this. A stimulus brings forth a certain response. By presenting two stimuli at the same time, conditioning takes place, so that the second stimulus will bring forth the original response. Remember that the child heard himself say "da." This served as a stimulus for him to repeat "da." When this stimulus-response pattern is well established, the second stimulus is introduced: at the same time he says "da" you say "da." Through conditioning, the child learns to respond to your stimulus as he had to his own, so when you say "da" he echoes, or responds with "da."

Let's carry this a step further. Every time that the child says "da" you show him a doll and repeat the syllable "da." Through the presentation of the visual stimulus (the doll) with the audible stimulus (the spoken "da") the two become associated, so that the sight of the doll serves as the stimulus for the child to say "da."

At this age "da" is quite satisfactory as the pronunciation of "doll." When the association is firmly established, we may start saying "doll" when he says "da." For example, when he holds out his hands and says "da," we may give him the doll and say, "Here is your doll." But we won't worry about his failure to use the sound of *l* for quite a while yet. We'll discuss that in the next chapter, but now let's go back to the stages of speech development.

During this stage called echolalia, he is building by imitation a repertoire of sounds and sound combinations that are peculiar to the language of his parents and environment. He must be able to produce these sounds voluntarily before he will be able to "speak" in the adult sense.

With this practice in imitation, an increasing interest in his environment, and better muscular control, the stage is set for his first real speech.

e. *True Speech*. The first word! How eagerly we wait for it! Already he has said "mama" and "dada," but these were the result of mere accident (lalling) or of imitation (echolalia). We can't honestly claim that he has spoken a true word until he does so consciously and with purpose.

When does this happen? "The average child" really begins to talk somewhere between 12 and 18 months of age. Of course there is no *average child*. There are many, many children—each with his own rate of development, each with his own environment which may furnish much or little stimulation toward speech. If we take the numbers 8, 9, 11, and 12, we say the "average is 10"—even though "10" does not actually occur in the series. So it is with the "average child." He's a figment of the imagination—a nonentity existing only in the computations of statisticians.

Some children begin to talk a month or two earlier than the average; others—just as normal—are content to wait a while longer before starting to talk. If he is a happy, healthy baby, if he uses sounds as well as gestures in his efforts to communicate, and if he gives evidence that he hears, we need not be concerned if he doesn't use true speech just yet.

Some children use no intelligible words until they suddenly and surprisingly produce a complete sentence. One four year old boy had distressed his parents by refusing to even say "mama" or "dada," "ball" or "drink." One afternoon he was taken to the zoo where he seemed especially interested in various birds. That evening when his mother was getting him ready for bed, she "almost fell off the Christmas tree" (to quote her) when her offspring said, "Muver, uh 'itto owl had feavers on its feet."

There are other instances of children who have used no speech *in the presence of their elders* until they uttered a complete sentence (although they must have been practicing when they were alone). These are, of course, unusual cases. They are referred to here only to emphasize the point that **children vary widely in the rate at which they acquire speech and the age at which they begin to talk.**

Later, we'll discuss when we should become concerned about the absence of speech. Right now, let's go back to the mythical "average child" and his first word.

As has been said, we cannot call the sounds he utters "speech" unless he uses conventional words intentionally and with purpose. That is, his actions must indicate that he expects a response that is appropriate to the situation *and* to the words he has spoken.

Before he can use words as the tools of communication he must know what they mean. Usually he will show that he understands quite a number of words before he begins to use any. He will shake his head or nod and start for the kitchen when you ask, "Do you want a drink?" long before he will say, "I want a dink." In fact, right on through the speech learning period his understanding of speech will exceed his use of speech. For that matter, most of us can hear or read and comprehend words that we never use.

About this time he suddenly becomes a very "human" member of the family. He learns to walk, to feed himself, and to talk—three mighty important developments. In fact, he's quite a person.

Before you lose patience with him, suppose you tackle the job of mastering even half as many new skills as he is acquiring!

At any rate, somewhere between 12 and 18 months of age, he'll probably begin to talk. His first words will not be pronounced precisely as we pronounce them. If he gives a "reasonable facsimile" and indicates that he is doing so "deliberately and with intent" we can be happy. If he consistently says "dah" for "doll" and "wah-wah" for "water" he's on the right track. At this early stage he has neither the articulatory skill to imitate exactly, nor the acoustic discernment to evaluate his own attempts. Let's not be unreasonable in the standards we set for him.

As he matures, as he gains more precise control of the muscles of articulation, as he develops increased auditory acuity (that is, sharper awareness of sounds that he hears), as he acquires the capacity for self-criticism, he will gradually acquire more skill at imitation. Accordingly, we may gradually raise our standards. We'll have more to say about this in the next chapter.

2. When should I worry?

Sometimes parents ask, "When should I begin to worry about my child's failure to acquire speech?" I'm always tempted to point out that worry doesn't solve problems; it only creates tensions and anxieties that complicate the problems.

If your child has gone through the babbling and lalling stages described in preceding pages, if his development in other respects (such as creeping and walking) is about what you should expect, if he is happy, healthy, and alert, and if you are sure that he can hear, you are probably safe in waiting until he is 30 months old before you seek help or advice.

As a matter of fact, some children who mature into normal adults do not begin to speak until the age of three years or even later. In the next chapter we'll discuss some of the reasons why a normal child may be late in acquiring speech, and some other possible causes of delay that are not so normal.

Some authorities would advise you not to become concerned until the child is three or three and a half years old. But it seems to me that by waiting this long we are running the risk of losing valuable time. If there is no reason for concern, I'd want to know that there wasn't. If there is some cause for concern, I'd want to know what is wrong and what ought to be done. If he needs medical care, I want him to have it. If in spite of my good intentions I've not been helping him as I should, I'd certainly want to know that, and find out what I should do.

For these reasons, if the child is not starting to use true speech (not speech that is perfectly articulated or pronounced, but speech that is purposeful and is a "reasonable facsimile" of conventional words) by the time he is 30 months old, a qualified speech correctionist should be consulted.

3. What will a speech correctionist do?

In order to reach some conclusion as to the nature, extent, and cause of the child's speech problem, the speech correctionist will need to know a great deal about the child and the home in which he lives. There will be questions about the mother's health during pregnancy, the child's health at birth, his early development, accidents and diseases. Perhaps none of the questions asked will reveal information that explains the difficulty, but we can't afford to overlook anything when we are dealing with so important a matter as your child's ability to communicate.

Figure 2: A speech correctionist will try to determine the nature and cause of the child's problem. Picture cards and objects will be used to evaluate the child's ability to produce the sounds of speech.

The speech correctionist will use a number of techniques to determine what sounds your child uses and what sounds he is able to produce. He will examine the "speech mechanism" to determine if any malformation is present and whether the nerves and muscles of the lips, tongue, and palate are functioning adequately for the production of speech. He will try to determine whether your child's hearing is impaired in such a way as to interfere with the learning of speech. If there is a problem, he will try to determine just what it is, what caused it, and what needs to be done.

He may tell you to continue exactly as you have been doing and to come back in six months if the child has not begun to speak. He may offer suggestions for helping your child learn to speak. Or he may discover something you have not been aware of that should have medical or surgical treatment. (In that case, he will refer you to your family physician or pediatrician.) At any rate, you would have the opinion of an expert in the field of speech, and—if you followed his suggestions—you would have the satisfaction of knowing that you were doing all you could to help your child toward the attainment of this important goal.

4. What could cause his delayed speech development?

Writers in the field of speech correction list 307 factors that may contribute to delayed speech development. As we consider any one child, it is usually rather easy to rule out many of these factors, but it is often difficult to conclude that any one factor is *the* cause of the problem. As a rule, a speech problem has several contributing causes.

Some of the more common causes of delayed speech development are also causes of articulation problems. We won't list all 307 possible causes, but some of the more common ones are discussed in Chapter III: Problems of Articulation.

5. What can I do to help?

Perhaps you are the parent of an infant and just want to be sure that you "don't do the wrong thing" or that you do all that you can "to make it easier." Or perhaps you are mildly concerned because your child is not beginning to talk. In any case, here are some suggestions. Here are some things that may be done to help a child learn to talk.

DON'T INTERRUPT. Remember that the first oral activity is undifferentiated crying which is part of his total response to a stimulus. Then he reaches the babbling stage where he experiments with sounds. When you hear him experimenting, you may be sure that he is comfortable and happy. Leave him alone! Listen to him. Try to keep a list of the sounds he uses. But don't interrupt him. Let him get this practice and experience. Let him become aware of the sounds he can make. Babbling is important for him, and he will do more of it if you don't rush in to join in his play everytime you hear him.

Have you noticed how talk at a dinner party gains momentum after the meal? Babies, too, will use the period after they are fed for vocal play if we do not subject them to a barrage of confusing and distracting stimuli. Hold him, sing to him, talk to him—but when he starts to babble, don't interrupt him. Use simple words and short phrases accompanied by gestures. Be consistent in vocalizations during eating, lifting, bathing, and other activities. This will help him identify certain sounds or words with certain activities. But give him time for his vocal play.

PROVIDE PROPER STIMULATION AT THE PROPER TIME. It is a mistake to try to stimulate imitation before the child is ready for it. Not until he has had the practice that babbling affords, and the experience of imitating himself that he finds in lalling—not until he has had both of these experiences will he be ready to imitate you.

There are two "secrets" or "tricks of the trade." First, get the baby to imitate your behavior before you try to get him to imitate your speech. Second, imitate the baby's speech if you want him to imitate yours. Sounds silly? Well, let's see how it works.

About the ninth month or soon thereafter the baby will be ready to imitate. Begin by joining him in a rhythmic activity that he is happily repeating. Perhaps he is banging his toy on the floor. Take the toy, bang it on the floor in the rhythm he was using; then put it back in his hand or where he can reach it. If he is ready for imitation he will take the toy and bang some more. Then it's your turn again. Watch his wide-eyed admiration of anyone so clever!

Play the game over and over. Clap your hands immediately after he claps his. Play peek-a-boo. He'll think you are fascinatingly clever if you can do the interesting things that he does. But don't rush him. Give him several seconds in which to respond. His reactions are not as fast as yours, and besides, this is all new to him. His interest span is short, so don't try to prolong an activity when he tires of it (no matter how much *you* are enjoying it!) .

Soon after he is old enough to enjoy the game of imitating activities, he will be ready for the next step—vocal imitation. When he's repeating a syllable over and over, interrupt him by softly repeating the same syllable. He will probably look at you with a mixture of curiosity and admiration, then continue making the sound. Here again, give him time! Wait a few seconds, then if he has not responded, repeat the same syllable softly several times. If he does not continue the game it is probably a sign that he is not quite ready for it. In that case, continue the game of imitating activities. But when he does begin to respond to vocal imitation his interest will grow rapidly, especially if he is rewarded with praise and affection so that the whole experience is a happy one for him.

Of course, once he has started to imitate, you will not make the mistake of interrupting his feeding to try to get him to say "bye-bye" to a departing guest. Nor will you rouse him from his nap to demonstrate his new skill for grandma who "would love to see him but can stay only a minute." These first lessons should be confined to the times when he enjoys his vocal play.

But don't overdo it! Too much stimulation is as bad for the child as too little. A few short periods a day will suffice.

Use Simple Words. After you have engaged in the game of imitating his oral sounds for a time, try giving him a single one-syllable word. He will be more apt to imitate you if the word is composed of sounds that he has practiced recently. And the sounds should be clearly visible—that is, produced by movements of the lips and tip of the tongue so that the child can see what you do. (Look in the mirror, and you'll discover that *put* is much easier to "see" than *cut*.)

Next, double syllables (ma-ma, da-da) may be attempted. After he has learned to imitate simple words and begins to show an interest in the names of objects, true disyllables may be used such as "water" in place of "wa-wa."

Some parents, having been warned of the evils of "baby-talk," make the mistake of trying to insist that the child say "mother," "father" etc. Well, baby-talk is all right for babies! At this step, "mama" is quite an achievement, and if the ball is consistently referred to as "bah" praise is in order. Don't confuse him with such gibberish as "Does-um-itto-precious-wantum-ball?" (Baby-talk is all right for *babies!*)

MOTIVATE HIM. Not only should the child hear plenty of speech, he must be motivated to use it. Speech is a tool for communication. The sooner the child learns this and begins to use it, even though imperfectly, the sooner he will begin to acquire good speech patterns. Anticipating the child's every wish makes speech unnecessary. If he has everything he wants, why should he make the effort to communicate? He should be encouraged to communicate vocally, and his efforts should be rewarded. If he begins to talk, you can help him to see the advantage of using better (or at least more conventional) pronunciation—but that should come later. Now, when he says, "Bah!" the ball should be given to him. It may be a good idea for you to say, "Here is the ba*ll*," for that is the way we want him to pronounce the word eventually. But many children do not master the *l* sound until they are six and a half years old. Let's not be unreasonable.

Sometimes a well-meaning neighbor may suggest, "Don't give him what he wants until he asks for it." That is a drastic step, and it may have serious consequences. Such a measure should be tried only if it has been recommended by a qualified speech correctionist who knows your child and you. The point being stressed here is that a child should be motivated to use his voice to communicate. He should be encouraged to make vocal sounds and should be rewarded for using them in his efforts to communicate.

USE SIMPLE SENTENCES. Most children will use one word to represent a complete thought or sentence. "Bah" may mean: "Where is my pretty red ball?" or "I dropped my ball." or "Do you want my ball?" Or it may mean, "Give me my ball and be quick about it!"

We may take our cue from the child and use short, simple sentences. He will come to understand us more quickly if we do. It is easier still for him to understand if we accompany these simple sentences with appropriate gestures and facial expressions.

Again, consider your learning of a foreign language. If we hear, "Levantaos!" accompanied by an appropriate gesture, we don't need to know Spanish to understand the command, "Get up!" But if this word were not accompanied by gestures and were lost in the middle of a complex sentence rapidly spoken, we'd have to be good students of Spanish to interpret it.

So, let's use single words or very simple phrases, accompanied by gestures and facial expressions.

Be Consistent. If "Levantaos" were repeated often enough in a situation that we understood, we'd learn to respond appropriately without the help of gestures. We would, in time, reach the place where we could recognize it as the key word in a longer sentence. But if many synonyms were used our problem would be more difficult.

We can help the child by being consistent, for he, too, will learn by associating the same words, gestures, and facial expression with the same activity. When we are going to feed the infant, let's use the same words over and over—spoken slowly and distinctly. The same with his bath or his preparations for bed.

If we bombard him with a confusing stream of synonyms, adverbs and adjectives, further confused by terms of endearment which may give satisfaction to us but have no meaning for him, we only complicate his already difficult problem and so delay the process of learning speech.

How much better it would be to concentrate on a few simple words and build up strong associations for them. Remember, he must understand speech before he can begin to use it, and we can help him to understand by consistently using the same phrases in the same situations.

6. Should I correct his errors?

That's a good question! But it's difficult to answer without knowing more about the child. Let's consider four cases. Assume that all four children have good hearing; they have developed quite normally in other ways (weaning, sitting, walking, etc.) , but you are concerned about their speech.

A is for Allen, who is 30 months old. He seems to understand what you say to him, but he doesn't try to talk to you. If he can't make you understand with gestures, he just gives up. Recommendation: Take him to a professionally prepared speech correctionist for consultation.

B is for Bobby. He, too, is 30 months old and seems to understand what you say to him. He calls "mama" quite understandably when he wants you, and he says "no" distinctly. He comes to you with a toy or a picture and jabbers away, but you can't understand a word he says. Recommendation: Consult a professionally prepared speech correctionist.

C is for Carol. She is three years old. *You* can understand a good deal of what she says, but you are worried because your next-door neighbor says with exasperation, "That child! I can't understand a word she says!" Recommendation: Read the next two chapters. If you are still concerned, take her to a qualified speech correctionist.

D is for David. He is five years old. He seems to be happy and "smart enough," but he says "tootie" for "cooky" and "fum" for "thumb." Recommendation: Correct his pronunciation of "cooky" but don't worry about "thumb" for a while yet.

The first part of Chapter III will explain why you would correct one word but not the other, and the rest of the chapter is devoted to describing what you can do to help. Right here we'll take time to say only: It is better to do nothing to correct your child than to go about correcting him in the wrong way.

7. How should I correct him?

Before answering that question, a word of caution is in order. You'll want to be sure that you are not demanding a sound that he isn't ready to make. Children master or acquire the sounds of speech in a rather definite sequence. We won't want to insist that a five year old produce a sound that the average child doesn't master until he is six or seven. (See the Articulation Chart on page 29.)

One father, a certified public accountant, brought his four year old son to the clinic because "He won't say statistics." In the first place, he was being unreasonable in expecting the four-year-old to produce the *s* sound. Some four-year-olds use a good *s*, but so many children have difficulty in mastering this sound that it appears in our chart at the seven-and-a-half year level! In the second place, many adults have difficulty with the word "statistics;" I know some public speakers who carefully avoid it. Let's be sure, then, that the sound we are demanding is a sound that he should be mastering at his age and level of development.

The first step in correcting the child is to help him hear the difference between the sound he used and the sound you want him to use. It won't do much good to say, "Don't say *tootie,* say *cooky.*" Many times the child does not hear the difference. Some children are faster than others, but all children require some time to develop sufficient hearing acuity or "ears that are sharp enough" to hear the difference between sounds that are acoustically similar.

Recently, in a garage, I heard a mechanic say, "Hand me that half-inch wrench." His helper handed him a wrench from a slot that was clearly marked "1/2." Without even trying the wrench to see if it would fit, the mechanic tossed it back and said, "That's a 7/16." Visually, the mechanic could detect much smaller differences than either his helper or I could. You might say he had "sharper eyes." We need to help the child develop "sharper ears" so that he can detect slight differences.

In an adult speech class I corrected a school teacher by saying, "The word is *wish.*" She looked at me in surprise and replied, "I said *wush.*" Odd, isn't it, that she didn't hear the difference. But she didn't! And it would have done no good to scold her. I had to help her hear the difference.

Talking to a group of parents, I asked them to repeat the nonsense word "tapataba." I had to repeat it several times slowly and distinctly before all of them could say it. I asked them to say it several times, then I said quickly, "Don't say tapataba, say tapadaba." One father in the group said it immediately. The others all looked at him and at me with puzzled expressions. They hadn't heard the difference.

The point is, we shouldn't expect the child to accomplish the difficult task of analyzing the word, selecting the incorrect sound, and substituting the correct sound without considerable help. We'll want to be sure that our request is reasonable and that the child understands what we expect of him. In other words, he must be able to hear the difference.

The conversation might go something like this:

Child: I want a tootie.

Parent: Here is your *cooky*. (Putting slight emphasis on the two *k* sounds. Then, while Johnny enjoys the cooky, you continue.) You know, Johnny, you don't say that word *cooky* exactly like grown-ups do. You say *tootie* and I say *cooky*. You start the word with the tick-tock sound t-t-t-t. That's what the clock says, isn't it? t-t-t-t. But this word starts with the cough sound k-k-k-k. Can you hear it when I say *cooky*? Listen: k-k-k-k. Can you make the cough sound k-k? That's fine. Let's both make the cough sound: k-k-k. Now say koo-koo-koo. Good boy. Now say key-key-key. That's it. Now let's put them together, like this: coo-key, coo-key. You try it. Good boy. Would you like another cooky?" (He has earned it!)

This type of correction takes more time and patience and ingenuity than "Don't say *tootie,* say *cooky*." But it will bring about results that are worth the extra trouble.

Of course, simply because he said "cooky" correctly a time or two does not mean that he will never again say "tootie."Well established habits are not easily discarded.

Recently, while my car was in the garage for extensive repairs, I was given the use of a car with a clutch—which I hadn't used for years. I stalled the engine at the first six stop lights! I kept forgetting to use the clutch. Now, I knew what to do, and I was perfectly capable of doing it. But I was watching traffic, intent on reaching my destination, and I forgot! Nobody wants to drive with all of his attention on the thought: Remember to use the clutch! During the week, using the clutch became habitual—I did it without thinking about it—automatically. Then I got my own car back, and for several days whenever I was thinking about where I was going rather than the mechanics of driving, I waved my left foot around trying to find the clutch.

The mechanics of speech are quite "automatic"—we don't stop to think: "The word *can* is composed of three phonetic elements. The first of these is formed by parting the lips, dropping the jaw slightly, lowering the tip of the tongue, lifting the back of the tongue to form a contact with the palate, building up a little breath pressure back of this closure, then dropping the tongue to release a puff of air. The second phonetic element of the word I want to say is—" We don't do any of that. We just say *can*. If speech required that much conscious effort it would certainly cut down on our idle chatter, wouldn't it?

Well, the child has his mind on *the cooky,* rather than on the new way that you want him to say *cooky,* and he is very apt to use his old speech pattern of *tootie.*

Before you become impatient with him, try this little experiment. Don't use any *l* sounds. Substitute a *d* sound instead. This will be easier for you than it is for the child to say *cooky,* for you already know the sound of *d* and can say "heddo" just as easily as you can say "hello." As long as you concentrate on using the sound of *d* instead of the sound of *l* you'll "get adong ad right." But as soon as you start thinking about what you are saying, more than likely you'll start using the *l* sound again in the familiar patterns.

Moral: You'll need to help him say the word correctly more than once—many times more.

Of course such correction should be done at appropriate times —don't humiliate him in the presence of others, don't try to correct him when he is excited or under emotional pressure, and don't spoil every experience for him by constant correction. Certainly, any attempt at correction should be done without emotion. As adults, we know that it's simply part of the learning process, and with the help that we owe him, he'll gradually eliminate errors and acquire acceptable patterns of speech. In Chapter III we'll discuss in greater detail the various steps or procedures you may follow in helping a child who has a problem of articulation. But now, while we are simply helping a child develop good speech patterns, we will want to render only such help as the child welcomes, and render it in a spirit of fun and good humor.

conclusion

Parents who do not know what to look for in their children's oral activities miss a great deal of enjoyment. As you watch your child develop through the various stages of acquiring speech, why not keep a list of the sounds he uses? See if he does not use more variety of sounds in his non-crying vocalizations than in his crying. Observe how he follows the general pattern described and help him in the mastery of the important skill you are so eager for him to acquire.

But remember, each child will have his own rate of development which may be faster or slower than the norms set forth in our discussion. You can help him most by being aware of his advance from one stage to the next (although there will be considerable overlapping) and using the type of stimulation that will be most helpful at each stage.

With proper teaching, many children will avoid the handicap of retarded or imperfect speech. But if your child should show signs of delayed speech development, consult a qualified speech correctionist. That's the only way you can be sure that you are doing all that you can to give your child the advantage of good speech!

chapter iii

62415

problems of articulation

YOU RECALL THAT THERE are three types of articulation problems: (1) omission of sounds (the child says "op" instead of "hop," "li'l" instead of "little," etc.), (2) substitution of sounds (the child says "thun" for "sun," "mudder" for "mother," etc.), and (3) distortion of sounds (the child "comes close" to the correct sound, but it isn't quite right). Before discussing how we can help a child who has a problem of articulation, let us consider two questions.

1. How can I tell if a child has a problem of articulation?

Does the child say "wabbit"? (rabbit)
Does the child say "tootie"? (cookie)
Does the child say "thoup"? (soup)

If he does, whether he has a speech problem depends on his age; for the sounds of speech are acquired or learned in a rather definite sequence.

In the following chart, you will find the ages by which the various sounds of speech *should* be mastered. Let us look at it before we go further.

ARTICULATION CHART		
Age	*Speech Sounds*	*Sample Words*
3½	p, b, m, h, w	*p*apa, *b*aby, *m*ama, *h*igh, *w*e
4½	t, d, n, k, g, ng, y	*t*o, *d*o, *n*o, *k*itty, *g*o wi*ng*, *y*et
5½	f	*f*un
6½	v, th (voiced) sh, zh, l	T.*V*., mo*th*er *sh*oe. trea*s*ure*, *l*ike
7½	ch, j, s, z th (voiceless), r, wh	*ch*air, *j*ump, *s*ee, *z*oo ba*th*, *r*ed, *wh*ere

*Note that the spelling does not always indicate the pronunciation. The *zh* sound is found in trea*s*ure; the *y* sound is found in on*i*on; and the *sh* sound is found in na*t*ion. See pages 44-45.

Some children will master sounds earlier than the age shown in the chart. But if a child has not mastered a sound by the time he has reached the age indicated, he may be considered retarded, to some extent, at least, in speech development. Of course, if a child lags a few months behind this schedule, we will not be unduly alarmed. For example, if a five-year-old uses all of the sounds that the chart shows he should have mastered with the exception of the *k* sound, we will give him a little more time and a little extra help before we become anxious about him. If he lags farther behind, there is more reason to be concerned. For another example, a seven-year-old makes the following errors: "dat" for "that," "mudder" for "mother," "tootie" for "cookie," "bud" for "bug." By looking at the chart, we see that the voiced *th* sound should have been mastered by the time he was $6\frac{1}{2}$; the *k* and *g* sounds, by the time he was $4\frac{1}{2}$. This child has a much more severe problem, and we will want to waste no time in seeking professional help.

The main reason for presenting the chart is to reassure you that "bah" or "baw" is an acceptable pronunciation of the word "ball" for a four- or five-year-old. Many children of his age can use the *l* sound, but so many are not able to use this sound until they are six or six and a half that we will not be upset by a five-year-old's failure to use a good *l* sound. We will not expect him to say "strawberry ice cream soda" for quite a while yet. You see, the *s* sound frequently is not mastered until the child is seven and a half years old.

Before starting to correct a sound, we want to be sure that the child is old enough for us to expect it of him. Better look at the chart again!

2. What causes an articulation problem?

Authors in this field list 307 factors that may contribute to a functional speech problem—that is, a speech problem for which there appears to be no physiological explanation. Seldom do we have a single cause. Usually there are several factors that combine to account for the defective speech. In this brief space we cannot discuss so complicated a problem with any degree of adequacy, but listed below are some of the more common causes:

a. *Lack of stimulation or motivation.* If a child is not talked to, sung to, and played with, he may not have much opportunity to learn to talk. If a child is waited on, with all of his wants anticipated, he may not have a need for speech. If his efforts at talking are ignored, rather than encouraged, he may feel that speech is not worth the effort.

b. *Hearing loss.* If a child cannot hear speech, he will not learn to talk in the normal way. It is possible for a child to be able to hear enough sounds so that he appears to "hear all right," and yet have a type of hearing loss that prevents him from hearing *all* of the speech sounds. In the section on hearing problems, this will be discussed further. The point to stress now is: if a child is slow in learning to talk, be sure that he can hear. The only way to be sure is to have his hearing checked by a competent person using an audiometer.

c. *Retarded mental development.* Although the presence of a speech defect is *not* an indication of mental retardation, children who are retarded or handicapped mentally are usually slow in learning to talk.

d. *Speech models that are poor.* Imitation plays an important part in learning to talk. The child should not be expected to develop speech that is better than the models that he is imitating. If an adult who takes care of the child's needs uses imperfect speech, talks in a whiny, nasal voice, or talks indistinctly (runningallthewordstogether) the child may be expected to do the same.

e. *Speech standards that are too high.* If the adults talking to the child use long words and complicated sentences, a child with his limited memory span and immature neurological-muscular development finds it impossible to imitate them. To encourage children to learn to talk, we should talk to them in simple phrases or one-word sentences, being sure to speak distinctly. We may take a lesson from the child on this point. When he says, "Baw" (which is quite acceptable for a child of 3 or 4 years), he may mean, "See the pretty red ball bounce," or "Where is my beautiful green and yellow ball?" or "Give me back my ball, you big bully." Instead of saying to the child in his play-pen, "Would my little darling like for his ever-loving mother to give him the ball to play with?," it would be better to simply hold out the ball and ask, "Ball?." That way his attention is focused on the one word and he will learn it much more quickly. "Want ball?" might come a little later, and "Do you want the ball?" later still.

f. *Constitutional factors.* Because the tongue and lips are extremely flexibile, considerable deviation in the structure of the oral cavity, the lips, teeth, and tongue may exist without preventing good speech. However, open-bite, widely spaced teeth, or other unusual conditions may make good speech difficult. Lack of coordination of the muscles of the lips, tongue, or soft palate will interfere with good articulation. A cleft palate or cleft lip will obviously present difficulties. Occasionally a child is "tongue-tied," but if a child has had no difficulty in nursing, if he can touch his lips with his tongue, and can lift the tip of the tongue to touch the gum ridge of the upper teeth, he is not "tongue-tied" in so far as speech is concerned. Although any marked deviation from the normal structure and function of the speech mechanism may make clear articulation more difficult, such deviation is more often a complicating factor than the sole cause of a speech problem.

suggestions for helping the child with a problem of articulation

We have said that if a child omits a sound (saying "ed" for "said" or "top" for "stop"), substitutes one sound for another (saying "muver" for "mother"), or distorts sounds (so that his speech is indistinct), he has an articulatory problem, provided that, as indicated on the Articulation Chart (Page 29), he is old enough to have mastered the use of the sound in question.

Speech is normally learned by imitation. Since we learn better when we are enjoying ourselves, speech sounds may best be presented for learning or relearning through humor and games. This is particularly true for young children. It is a good idea to have a child listen to the sounds of animals and nature and then try to reproduce them. By so doing, we encourage an interest in and an awareness of sound. Play games with him in which you imitate the sound of a howling wind, a slamming door, a barking dog, a cat, a cow, a pig, and other familiar sounds.

It is probably inaccurate to say that children "outgrow" speech defects. Speech is the result of learning, of developing skill in listening and discrimination, of developing skills in precise neuro-muscular control. While it is true that some children overcome their difficulties through blundering methods of self-help, many do not. All children will improve their speech more rapidly if they receive carefully planned help. Often a little assistance will help a child avoid the stigma of being "different" or of being called "babyish."

Of course, you will want to be sure that there is nothing physically wrong with your child. The first thing to do is to consult your doctor or a qualified speech correctionist to be sure that there is no physical reason for the poor speech. Then, too, you will want to make certain that he has good hearing—a child cannot imitate a sound that he cannot hear. An important point to remember is that even though your child responds to sound and comes when you call, he may have a hearing loss that prevents his hearing all of the sounds of speech. The importance of a hearing test administered by a professional person using an audiometer cannot be stressed too much.

Because each child is an individual, the therapy or "speech training" should be adapted to his needs, interests, and abilities. However, there are some procedures that may generally be followed.

Prerequisites

Before we talk about procedures, let's talk a little bit about the person who is going to help the child. Here are a few "musts."

1. *There must be a good relationship* between the child and his helper or teacher. If one does not like the other and enjoy being with him or her, there's not much point in starting.

2. *You must be pleasant.* Remember, speech is a means of communication. If what we communicate is not pleasant, we'd rather do without it. If a pleasant atmosphere can be created between "pupil" and "teacher," you have taken an important step.

3. *You must be patient.* Remember, speech is complex and difficult. If the child did not need your patient help and encouragement he would already be talking acceptably. Progress, in most instance, will be slow. Most of us learn by "fits and starts." In other words, he will probably do well for a while, then seemingly make

no progress for a time. This lack of progress may be just as frustrating to him as it is to you. During these times, he will especially need your patience, encouragement, and confidence.

4. *You must be accepting.* This is another way of saying that you must love the child just as he is—speech defect included. Of course, you must not expect any better speech than he is able to produce. In fact, to be realistic and not to hold higher standards for the child than we hold for ourselves, we should accept and approve of speech that is not quite as good as he is able to produce. (For just among us adults, not many of us *always* perform at our best, do we?)

Sometimes, because of anxieties and antagonisms that have been built up around the speech defect, a favorite aunt or uncle may be in a more advantageous position than the parents to serve as the "speech helper."

Now that the stage is set, let's consider some of the procedures that will be effective with the majority of articulation cases, remembering that before the program is initiated, you should have consulted with a qualified speech correctionist.

Procedures

Although the amount of time devoted to each step will vary from child to child, and from sound to sound with the same child, the following steps are involved in helping a child improve his articulation.

1. *Auditory training—learning to listen.*

   (a) The child must learn to recognize the correct sound and to distinguish it from other sounds. At first, the sounds must be so stressed that the difference is accentuated. Comparisons should be made between the sound to be taught and sounds that are markedly different. Gradually the stress may be reduced, and as skill in discrimination is developed, comparison may be made between sounds that are similar. The goal of this step is to enable the child to readily distinguish between the incorrect sound he has been using and the correct sound that we want him to use.

   (b) The next step is for the child to learn to identify—to "pick this sound out"—when it is used in a word, and to distinguish it from other sounds. Again, the sounds should be stressed or prolonged to assist the child in identifying them. As skill is developed, stress or emphasis may be reduced. Usually a child uses a new sound at the beginning of a word before he uses it at the end of a word. Use of the sound in the middle of a word is ordinarily mastered last. In teaching the child to recognize a new sound, it is wise to follow this same procedure: presenting the sound first at the beginning of a word where it is most obvious. When this can be done easily, present the sound at the end of a word, and finally in the middle of words. Until the child can easily and consistently "pick out" the sound being taught and distinguish it from other sounds, we are not ready to proceed to the next step.

2. Learning how the sound is made.

Only a few speech sounds are produced with movements or placements that are clearly visible, so that the child can see how they are made. Some of the sounds with which children have major difficulty are produced in a manner that the child cannot observe. The lack of these visual cues may be one of the reasons for the difficulty. For most speech sounds, the child will have to find the target—that is, he will have to experiment. He will have to search not only for the precise placement of the lips, tongue, and palate, but for the exact and small movement that will produce the correct sound.

3. Making the sound easily and consistently.

At first, the production of the correct sound may be almost accidental—stumbled upon during the child's experimentation. The goal of this step is to provide enough practice so that the child can produce the sound without stopping to think about the movement or placement involved.

4. Using the new sound in nonsense syllables.

Most children find it easier to use "the new sound" in a new context than to substitute the new sound in place of the well-established error. That is, it is easier to learn a new combination of sounds (such as, "ra, ree, ri, ro, ru") than it is to use the *r* sound in the word "red" when you have habitually said "wed."

5. Using the new sound in a few familiar words.

After the child has learned to produce the correct consonant sound in combination with all of the vowels, he should be taught to use it in a few familiar words. Remember, as stated above, he will be able to use the new sound at the beginning of a word more easily than in any other position. After this can be done easily, he may be taught to use the new sound at the end of words, then in the middle of words.

6. Using the new sound in a nucleus situation.

Even after the child is able to make the new sound, and to correctly pronounce words containing the sound, he should not be expected to use it consistently. When he is excited, or in a hurry, or angry, or tired—he may be expected to slip back into the old, familiar habits of speech. None of us enjoys being "on our good behavior" all of the time. We get tired of "watching our p's and q's." We want to relax for a while and "just be ourselves." Remembering this, we can understand why the child will not be consistent in his use of the new sound.

You can make the sound of *w* just as easily as you can make the sound of *r*. Since you can use both of these sounds without conscious effort, it will be easier for you to substitute one for the other than it will be for the child to substitute the "new sound" for his old error. Suppose you try it. For the rest of the day, don't use the *r* sound, use the *w* sound instead. See how long it is before you slip back into the old pattern. You'd better have someone checking on you, just to be sure you don't use the *r* without thinking of it.

After this experiment, you'll be much more patient with the child who "can" but "doesn't" use the correct sound.

To help the child learn to use the new sound, without antagonizing him with frequent corrections that interrupt his story or his questions, it is wise to set up a "nucleus situation." Set aside a fifteen or twenty minute period (perhaps only ten minutes for the very young child), during which time the child knows that he will be corrected if he uses the wrong sound. As the number of corrections decreases, the time may be lengthened, or a second or third "good speech period" may be set up.

During the rest of the day, ignore his errors. Of course, if he corrects himself, he should be rewarded. A smile, a wink, a "Good boy!"—all are rewards that let the child know you are aware of his efforts to improve his speech and will encourage him to further efforts. As a matter of fact, when the child reaches the point where he can and does correct himself, the rockiest portion of the road has been covered.

7. *Using the sound habitually.*

The final goal of therapy is to make the use of the correct sound habitual. This means that he will use it spontaneously and without conscious effort.

Let's Be Specific

The procedures presented above may be more meaningful if we apply them to a specific case. Let's take a child who substitutes the *w* sound for the *r* sound. He says "wed" for "red," and "wabbit" for "rabbit." What shall we do?

1. *Auditory training.* First we must help the child learn to recognize the sound. We can't expect him to reproduce it unless he has heard it distinctly and has a clear-cut "auditory image" of what we want him to say.

No matter what sound we are working on, we must be sure to use the *sound,* not the name of the letter of the alphabet. In this case, we will want to make the sound of the *w* rather than say "double you." and we will use the sound of the *r* (pronounced "er" as heard at the beginning of "rah") rather than the name of the letter (pronounced "are").

To help him hear the difference, we might say something like this: "Billy, we don't say that word quite the same. You say 'wwwed' (prolonging the *w* sound) and I say 'rrrred' (prolonging the *r* sound). You begin that word with the wind sound: 'wwwww.' Make the wind sound: 'wwwww.' Good boy! Let's think of some words that begin with that sound: we, wind, wait, well. Let me hear you say 'we,' etc. Make the wind sound good and strong: 'wwwwe'."

Continuing, we might say, "Those words all begin with the wind

sound: 'wwwww.' But the word 'rrrred' begins with the growling
dog sound. Listen: 'rrrrr, rrrrr.' That's the growling dog sound;
'rrrrr'."

We do not ask the child to produce the *r* sound. Not yet! Just
now we want to be sure he can hear and recognize the *r* sound and
distinguish it from other sounds. We will use some games to be sure
that he can. Let him wave a white flag when he hears a *w* (the wind
sound) and wave a red flag when he hears an *r* (the growling dog
sound), or point to the picture of a dog, or pick up a block when he
hears the *r*. You can devise many "games" of this sort that will help
him learn to listen.

First then, he learns to distinguish between the sounds as they
are produced in isolation—that is, by themselves. Then he must
learn to tell the difference between the two sounds when they are
"hidden in words." When he is ready for this step, we might say,
"You know these sounds so well, now I'm going to make the game
more fun. You will have to hunt for the sound. I am going to hide
it in a word and see if you can find it." "Games" similar to those
above may be used if they are needed for the motivation of young
children. *Not until he can make this distinction easily are we ready
for the next step.*

2. *Help the child make the correct sound in isolation.* To try
this step, we might say, "You are very good at picking out the growling dog sound whenever you hear it. Listen carefully while I make
the sound. I will make the growling dog sound three times. Then I
want you to make it just once." By this method, we are providing
strong auditory stimulation. If he does not succeed the first trial, say,
"Now it's my turn to say it again." Stimulate him strongly, then
let him make another effort. After a few such trials, if he is still
unable to produce an acceptable *r* sound, go back to step 1 for further auditory training. If he does succeed in producing the correct
sound, we are ready for step 3.

3. *Have him practise making the sound.* If he produces the correct sound, we want to help him remember just how he did it. We
want to re-enforce and strengthen the production of the sound, so
that he may produce it easily and consistently. To do this, we will

use a variety of speech games, drills, and exercises. For example, he may move a block, or throw a dart, or take a step only when he produces a satisfactory *r* sound. Checkers, parchesi, or a game you improvise may serve as a vehicle for providing the needed practice. If the game involves a spinner, he may be required to produce a sustained *r* sound for as long as the pointer spins. The main thing is practice made as attractive as possible, without losing sight of the goal: producing a good "growling dog sound."

4. *Using the sound in nonsense syllables* will familiarize the child with the sound in combination with all vowel sounds. You don't have to be clever with rhymes to make up your own. For example:

> Ree, ri, ro, ray
>
> What do you say?
>
> Ree, ri, ro, ru
>
> It's up to you.

The child may be required to say the "magic words" before he can take his turn in the game. (Of course, the adult must follow the same rules!) When he can easily produce the *r* sound before a vowel (ree), after a vowel (oor), between two vowels (oroo, oree, iree, etc.), we are ready for step 5.

5. *We are now ready to help the child learn to use the "new sound"* in a few familiar words. The words chosen should be words that the child uses. You might begin by saying, "Let me hear you say 'ree'. . . . Good. Now let me hear you say 'roll.' (Be sure to stress the *r*.) Remember, we are working only on the one sound of *r*. If the child does not produce an *l* sound, we are not concerned about it here. After he masters the *r*, we may tackle another sound and follow similar procedures.

You may want to present the word "here." If he can use the *r* sound in these two words, you may further strengthen their production by using them in a game. For example, you could sit on the floor with a ball. You say, "*R*oll the ball." The child rolls it saying, "He*r*e it comes." Then the child says, "*R*oll the ball," etc. You will be able to think up many other ways of utilizing the words he can say correctly. If you teach the word "*r*ound," when you play a game with a spinner, the child may say, "Rrrround it goes," whenever he spins. As new words are added to the list, re-enforce them by using them.

Figure 3: When working with young children it is often desirable to combine speech correction with interesting activities. Improvement is usually more rapid when the father takes an active part in the "speech lessons."

Another helpful and (for most children) interesting activity may be introduced at this point: the making of "My Speech Book." Any kind of scrapbook may be used. At the top of the page, print the letter *r* and a picture of a growling dog may be pasted in to remind the child of the sound. Help the child find pictures of objects with names that include the *r* sound: rabbit, rope, radish, carrot, bedroom, horse, etc. You, or the child if he knows how, may print the appropriate word under each picture. After finding pictures (and this can be a part of preceding steps) , he is allowed to paste them in his speech book only when he can say them. Going back and naming pictures already in the book is good review.

Teachers often find that this "speech book" idea is helpful in their work with phonics. It stimulates an interest in printing or writing and spelling, as well as in "learning new sounds." Children may be allowed to draw their own pictures. If it looks like a walrus and he calls it a horse, don't criticize—just be glad he can say "horse."

Usually the child will be able to use a sound at the beginning of words before he can use it at the end or in the middle of words. Usually he will be able to use a sound as a single consonant, (*r*ope, *r*ip, *r*ipe, *r*at) before he can use it in blends, (*tr*ue, *dr*aw, *dr*ink, *cr*eam, *gr*ow). With the sound of *r*, however, a child frequently finds it easier to say the *tr* blend (as in *tr*ue) or the *dr* blend (as in *dr*aw) than to use the single consonant sound of *r* (as in *r*ope). If in working with the child, you find this to be true, by all means introduce the easier words first! Nothing will spur him on to greater effort than to find that he can use the sound correctly in some words.

6. *Use the new sound in a nucleus situation.* Set up a ten, fifteen, or twenty minute period during which the child knows that he will be corrected if he does not use his new sound. The length of this period will depend upon the age and attention span of the child—and upon your ingenuity! Usually it is wise to avoid using meal time. If the child is having difficulty so that you need to correct him often, the tension related to his speech may spread to the meal, and an eating problem may result. During this nucleus situation, or "good speech period," you may visit, play games, or go for a walk. You will not expect perfect speech. You will accept the best that the child can produce. In other words, you will correct only the errors in the sound being studied.

Nor does "correcting" mean that you interrupt the sentence and "pounce" on the error. Suppose he asks, "Is that *w*eally the way you go?" You would let him finish, then say, "Yes, that is *rrr*eally the way you go. Let me hear you say '*rrr*eally.' "

Ignore the "slips" during the rest of the day (no one likes to be nagged), but give praise when the child corrects his own errors. Even praise must be given judiciously. If he corrects himself in the presence of guests, a wink or a smile for him alone may be all the reward or praise that is needed. If you feel that some comment should be made, wait until you are alone. I recall the story of a boy whose mother went into ecstacy over his spelling paper marked "100." At first, the boy was pleased, but as the mother continued her song of praise, the boy interrupted to ask, "What's the matter, Mom? Didn't you think I could do it?" Praise is important. We want to have our successes and our efforts recognized. But don't overdo it.

7. *The last step is to help the child use the sound habitually.* This means "spontaneously and without conscious effort." Nucleus situations or "good speech periods" may be increased in length and there may be two or three a day. For a little variety, you might say, "Tonight let's surprise daddy at supper. How would you like to try using your new sound friend (or the growling dog sound) all the time we are at the table. You know how to say 'butter' and 'bread' and 'fork.' If you make a mistake, I won't say anything. I'll just reach up and pull my ear. That will be our secret signal. It will mean for you to say the sentence again." Usually children respond to this approach. "Secret signals" are fun, and your suggestion that he use the mealtime for a "good speech period" is a vote of confidence.

We haven't forgotten the caution concerning tensions at mealtime. You won't want to "surprise daddy at supper" until you are sure that the child will meet with reasonable success. Even then, if (unfortunately) meals are times of "stress and strain," you can just as well use some other time or situation; for example, while at the store, while Aunt Margaret is here, while visiting Uncle Ezra.

The steps outlined above are those usually followed in helping a child master a new sound. It is impossible to state how long each step will take. A great deal depends upon the child, the difficulty of the sound, and the manner in which each step is presented. Just don't get in too big a hurry. Of course, you are eager to have the child improve as rapidly as possible. But in this case, it is wise to "make haste slowly." Be sure that each step is mastered before moving on to the next. Don't hesitate to go back to an earlier step if the child is encountering too much difficulty and is losing interest. Progress is usually slow—so don't be discouraged.

More Helpful Hints

The suggestions given below may be of further help:

Present the sound while the child watches as well as listens.

Stimulate him with the repetition of the sound in a story or rhyme before asking him to produce it.

Let him watch and listen as you both face a mirror and call his attention to how the sound is produced.

To distinguish between voiced and voiceless sounds (such as *f* and *v*), have the child feel his larynx or voice box. You may wish to refer to it as "the voice motor." When the vocal folds vibrate (as for the *v* and other voiced sounds), the "motor is running," and he can feel the vibrations. Let him feel your "speech motor" as you show him the difference between the sound of *v* with the motor turned on, and *f* with the motor turned off. The teeth and lips remain in the same position. "Turning the motor on or off" makes the difference.

Work on one sound at a time. Work first on the sound that is normally acquired at the earliest age (see chart on page 29) or on the sound that is most easily seen. (The *t* should be easier to learn than the *k* because it is usually mastered at an earlier age. The *f* should be easier to learn than the *k* because you can *see how* it is made.)

Speech exercises should be fun. Create an atmosphere of play. Praise frequently—you can compliment the child for his effort even when he does not quite succeed. Just don't let the game become so exciting that you or the child forgets the purpose. For older children who are eager to improve their speech, the "fun" element is not as important, but even then the "speech lesson" should be pleasant.

If the child is tiring of one exercise or game, change to another. He will learn more readily when he is interested.

Frequent short lesson periods are more effective than a few long sessions. Father can help here! In fact, his cooperation is important throughout the program. Even a short session held regularly will be rewarding to both the father and the child.

Be sure to identify the sound, not by the name of the letter, but by the sound produced in a word. For example, when you see an *s*, you say, "That is the letter 'eh-sss'." The *name* of the letter has two sounds: "eh-sss." But in a word, the letter stands for only the second of these sounds, the "sss" as is heard in *s*oup. The name of the letter *r* is "ah-rrr," but when we see the letter in a word, we pronounce only the second part of its name, the "rrr." We do not say "ahrun," we say "run." We will not talk about the "eh-sss" sound, but about the "sss"; we will not ask the child to make an "ah-rrr" sound, but an "rrr" sound.

Prolonging and slightly stressing or exaggerating the sound is often helpful in the early steps of auditory training.

Be patient! Learning a new sound involves breaking down well-established neuro-muscular patterns and building up new ones. It is a complicated, difficult process.

Keep the child aware of his progress. Your goal for the child is good speech. But the child needs to have a goal that can more quickly be reached. Many different devices may be used. A common one is the "Speechometer" which the child may color as each step of the therapy is mastered. A copy of this motivating device is found facing this page.

Encourage the child to talk. Give him opportunities to take part in family discussions. Are you planning a picnic or a trip? Let him feel that he has a part in the plans. As he becomes aware of the importance of speech as a means of communication, he will be more willing to work for improvement.

In working with articulatory problems, it is often helpful to give the sound a little distinction or "personality." One method of doing this is to give the sound a special name. There are two reasons for doing this. First, it helps to identify the sound—to set it apart from others. Second, the use of "letter names" is confusing. A sound may be represented by a variety of spellings. For example, the "angry kitten sound" may be spelled *f* as in "fun," *ph* as in "phone," or *gh* as in "laugh." Then, too, the letters of the alphabet do not always represent the same sound. The *c* is pronounced as *s* in "cent," but as *k* in "cook." The *s* is pronounced as *s* in "sister," but as *z* in "is" and "was." Remember, it is the sound (not the letter) that is our concern. To avoid confusing the child, we use special names such as "the wind sound" for the *w* and "the growling dog sound" for the *r*. Other suggestions for naming sounds are given on pages 46-48.

Many times it is wise to begin our "speech lessons" by teaching a sound with which the child has no difficulty. There are several reasons for this procedure:

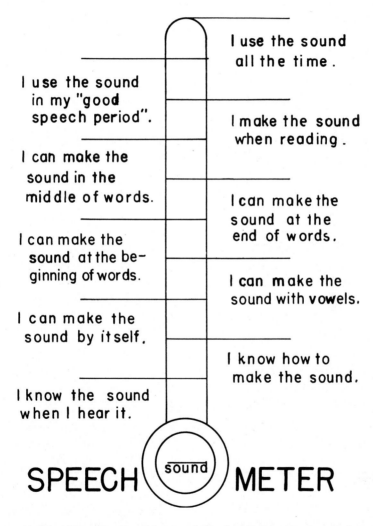

Figure 4: The "Speechometer" is one of the devices you may use to keep the child aware of his progress and to motivate him to further effort.

(1) It helps to establish a friendly relationship between teacher and pupil.

(2) It enables the child to become familiar with the techniques and terminology the teacher will use.

(3) It gives practice in "limbering up" the muscles of the tongue, lips, jaw, and palate and helps develop the rapid, precise movements essential for speech.

(4) It encourages the child. "Nothing succeeds like success." The child finds that these "speech lessons" are fun. He can do what he is asked to do. As a result, he is more willing to tackle the "new sound" and approaches it with greater confidence.

The list presented below presents the sounds in the order in which they are normally acquired by children. A special name is suggested for identifying the sound. Suggestions are made for producing the sound through imitation, and a helpful hint or two are given for the production of the sound. In the column headed "Additional Aids," you will find the phrase "motor running" or "motor not running." These terms are used to help the child distinguish between the voiced and unvoiced or voiceless sounds. A sound is "voiced" if the vocal folds in the larynx or voice box vibrate. The child can put his fingers on his throat and "feel the motor running." A sound is "unvoiced" or "voiceless" if the vocal folds do not vibrate. The child can feel no vibration in the voice box, "the motor is not running." For example, the *f* sound and the *v* sound are made in the same way (upper teeth resting lightly on lower lip) except that the "motor is not running" for the *f* and is "turned on" or "running" for the *v*.

SOUND	NAME	IMITATION	ADDITIONAL AIDS
p	motor boat	motor boat (p-p-p) baby chick (peep-peep) popcorn (pop-pop)	Lips shut, then suddenly release with puff of air. Motor not running.
b	sheep	sheep (baa-baa)	Same as *p*, except motor running.
m	mother mosquito	mosquito (m-m-m) humming top (m-m-m)	Lips shut, motor running. Feel buzz in nose.
h	laugh sound or panting puppy	laugh (ha-ha) panting (h-h-h)	Motor off, breath emitted through lips that are shaped for vowels which follow.

SOUND	NAME	IMITATION	ADDITIONAL AIDS
w	pig or wind	pig (wee-wee) wind (w-w-w-woo)	Lips rounded, back of tongue raised (similar to o͞o) .
t	watch sound	watch (t-t-t) clock (tick-tock)	Press tip of tongue against upper gum ridge. Release suddenly with explosive puff. Motor not running.
d	woodpecker	woodpecker (d-d-d)	Same as *t,* but with motor on.
n	baby mosquito	baby mosquito (n-n-n)	Tongue placed as for *t.* Hold position as air passes through nose with motor running. Feel hum in nose.
k	cough sound or duck	cough (k-k-k) quack crow (kaw-kaw)	Back of tongue raised against soft palate. Pull tongue away quickly to let air escape with explosive puff. Motor off.
g	frog	frog (g-g-g)	Same as *k,* but with motor running.
ng	bell or father mosquito	bell (ding-dong) ng (ring-ring)	Back of tongue raised against hard palate. Air passes through nose. Motor running. Feel hum in nose.
y	howling wind	wind (yoo) puppy (yipe)	Middle of tongue raised, tip lowered, teeth slightly separated. Motor is running. *Y* is a glide from the *ee* to the following vowel.
f	cross kitten	kitten spitting (f-f-f)	Place lower lip lightly against upper teeth. Push air out. Motor is not running.
sh	hush sound	hush (sh-sh) baby is sleeping	Tongue is pulled back slightly from teeth. Blow air through slightly protruded lips. Motor off.
v	fly sound	fly buzzing (v-v-v)	Same as *f* with motor turned on.
th (voiced) (as in *th*at)	airplane	airplane (th-th-th)	Top of tongue placed lightly against inside edge of upper teeth. Turn on motor and blow. Air exits over tip of tongue.

SOUND	NAME	IMITATION	ADDITIONAL AIDS
l	dial tone in telephone		Front of tongue pressed lightly against upper teeth ridge. Voice flows over lowered sides of tongue. Motor running.
s	teakettle or Sammy Snake	snake (s-s-s) air escaping from bicycle tire	Sides of tongue against upper gums, tip does not quite touch front teeth. Teeth together. Motor off. Sometimes easier to obtain moving to or from the *t* sound (st or ts)
z	bee	bee buzzing (z-z-z)	Same as *s* with motor running. (buzz in voice box)
ch	train	train (choo-choo) truck (chug-chug)	Tongue pressed against upper gums; draw tongue back to release quickly. A combination of *t* and *sh*. Motor off.
j	jumping jack	farm horse (jig-jog) (identify with "Jack and Jill")	Same as *ch* with motor on.
th (voiceless) (as in *thin*)	goose	goose (th-th) windmill (thh- - -)	Same as voiced *th*, but turn off motor.
r	growling dog or fire engine	growl (r-r-r-r) siren (r-r-r-r)	Spread lips in a smile. Sides of tongue raised to touch upper teeth. Turn on motor, *r* rolls down middle of tongue and out over the tip which is turned back slightly to form a hollow.
wh	pinwheel	whirring of pinwheel owl (whoo)	Lips rounded and protruded. Tongue raised in back, tip touches lower teeth. Teeth slightly separated. Motor off. *HW* would be a better spelling since a puff of air is emitted before the *w* is sounded.
q	has no sound of its own. It is another spelling for the *k* or cough sound.		
c	has no sound of its own. It is either *s* as in "city" or *k* as in "can".		
x	is a combination of *k* and *s* as in "tax" and "six", or *g* and *z* as in "exactly".		

There is nothing "magic" about this sequence, but children usually learn to use sounds in this order. Of course, if a child is able to say "yes," but says "thun" for "sun," the *s* sound may be isolated and identified, and the training proceed from this point. (See step 2 under Procedures on page 35.)

Usually it is wiser to delay teaching the blends (*bl*—"blue," *gr*—"green," *kw*—"queen," *ks*—"six," *pl*—"play," etc.) until the child can easily and consistently produce each of the sounds that make up the blend. Occasionally, a child may learn a blend before he can produce the components separately. In this case, we may help him to hear the components by saying them slowly and help him to separate them by giving each its name, then proceed with the steps of training already discussed.

If your child is working with a speech correctionist, you will, of course, want to use the "special names" that the correctionist uses. If you are working alone and find that the child responds better to some other name, by all means, use it. There is no magic in these names. The *s* sound might as well be the "teakettle sound" or "the punctured tire sound" as the "snake sound." The point is, a special name gives the sound some distinction and makes it easier to remember.

The production of a single speech sound involves the carefully timed stimulus of many muscles and their precise movement. It is complicated! So we will need patience and skill if we are to help the child. If these steps are patiently followed, you should find your reward in improved speech. The road will probably be rocky at times. The child will seem to accomplish one step quickly, but be very slow in achieving the next step. This is to be expected. Patience, enthusiasm, and ingenuity will produce results.

Good luck! and good speech!

chapter iv

stuttering and non-fluency

1. How can I tell if a child stutters?

IT IS NOT EASY TO answer this question without observing your child and hearing him talk. But here are some interesting facts.

Fact: The average adult speaker has from six to eight hesitations or "interruptions of fluency" per minute. Perfect fluency just is not found. Actors who have their lines memorized also memorize hesitations and repetitions in order to make their speech sound natural. Try listening to your neighbors. You will hear a number of "ums," "uhs," and "well-ahs." These are breaks in fluency. If adults with all of their experience have difficulty in expressing themselves fluently, what right do we have to expect perfect fluency of children?

Fact: Children between the ages of three and six years have an average of 49 repetitions of sounds, words, or phrases per 1,000 words of speech during free play. Some children whose speech develops "normally" repeat as many as ten per cent of their words.

Fact: All children have more repetitions in situations of stress or excitement than in free play.

Fact: For most young children, the diagnosis of stuttering is made by parents rather than by speech correctionists. This is an important point to remember for the following reason: research indicates that at the time Johnny's parents decide that he is stuttering, there is little or no difference between Johnny's speech and Tommy's, but *Tommy's parents accept his speech as normal* and are not concerned about it. Could it be that the difference is in the minds of the parents rather than in the speech of the child? At least the evidence points out the necessity for being reluctant to attach the label of "stuttering" to any child.

Fact: Once a child is judged by his parents to be a stutterer, his speech tends to become more hesitant and repetitious, and he tends to exhibit more tensions. He may be reacting to the anxiety of his parents about his speech. We know that children talk more freely in a relaxed, pleasant atmosphere. It seems that, in some cases at least, the anxiety of the parents about a perfectly normal lack of fluency causes the child to be overly concerned about his speech. The more he tries to please his parents, the more he tries to measure up to the standards expected of him, the more tense and anxious he becomes. The more tense he becomes, the more repetitions he has. The more repetitions he has, the greater the anxiety of the parents. The greater the anxiety of the parents. . . . This goes on and on in a vicious circle. All the more reason for just accepting his speech as it is. You don't blame him for having brown eyes instead of blue. You don't constantly fuss at him to make him grow taller. You don't scowl and show your disapproval because he has a cowlick. That's the way he is, and he's yours, and you're proud of him. Accept his speech in the same way and don't permit well-meaning neighbors or relatives to comment on his speech to the child or in the child's presence.

If, after reading this, you still think your child has more than his share of hesitations and repetitions, before you decide that he "stutters," listen to a group of children of the same age as your child. Do not compare him with his sister! Girls are faster in acquiring both vocabulary and fluency.

The chances are you will discover that other children (about whom you have not been concerned because they are not *yours*) have the same kind of difficulty as your child in expressing themselves.

If you are still concerned, consult a speech correctionist before you apply the label "stutterer" or permit anyone else to apply it.

2. *Why do young children have so many hesitations and repetitions?*

Let's suppose that you have studied Russian or Chinese for a while. You have learned how to say, "Good morning," "I want a drink," "Open the door," and a few other phrases. Then, suddenly, you are asked to talk in Russian or Chinese to express your opinion on an important subject. How fluent would you be? I don't know about you, but I know from experience with a foreign language that I would fumble, hesitate, start over—in fact, I would have all of the symptoms of stuttering. What's the matter? I just don't have the vocabulary. Lack of vocabulary and language facility are two important factors in accounting for a child's difficulty.

Jimmy or Sally comes running in and says, "Mama—Mama, I—I saw—a—a—there's a—a—it's a—I saw—saw—." Now the child knows what a bird is and knows what a bee is. But what the child wants you to hurry outdoors to see is too small to be a bird and too large to be a bee. It was a humming bird. But "humming bird" isn't in the child's vocabulary, so, of course, it can't be used to describe what was seen. The hesitations and repetitions are not symptoms of some strange and mysterious malady. They simply indicate that the child is having new experiences and doesn't have the vocabulary to describe them.

From age three to six, the typical child is encountering many new experiences. Some of them he only vaguely comprehends; they confuse him. He has neither the vocabulary nor the facility with language to express himself. We adults do the same thing when we try to talk about something we don't fully understand.

3. Are children apt to have more hesitations and repetitions in some situations than in others?

There are wide variations in fluency from one child to the next, and there are wide variations in the fluency of one child from situation to situation. Although individuals differ, children are apt to have more difficulty—that is, more breaks in fluency—when:
(1) They attempt to explain things they don't understand or for which they do not have adequate vocabulary.
(2) They are forced to compete with others in talking. At the dinner table when the whole family is talking; when he gets home from school and another brother or sister wants to tell the same story, to cite just two common situations.
(3) They are not sure that they have your attention; for example, when mother is intent on cutting out a dress, or when father's face is hidden by a newspaper.
(4) They are excited or upset. Common examples would be: when being punished, in the midst of an exciting game, entering a new

school, moving to a new neighborhood, during a tiring trip. He is especially apt to have difficulty if he does not understand why he is being punished or feels that the punishment is unfair.

(5) They are in the midst of inner or outer conflict. An example of inner conflict would be when you ask him, "Who broke this vase?" If he did, shall he tell the truth and receive your displeasure, or shall he lie—as you have taught him it is wrong to do? An example of outer conflict would be when he wants to do something other than what you or his playmates want him to do, or when he wants you or his playmates to do something other than you want to do.

(6) They are forced to speak in situations that are fearful or threatening. For example, you think it's "so cute" the way he says "ossifer" instead of "officer." You want him to say (so Aunt Susan can hear), "Daddy is an officer." He knows that if he tries it, he will be laughed at. Forcing him to talk in any situation in which he does not feel secure, in which he does not feel that he can succeed, is apt to be difficult for him. The result? More hesitations and repetitions.

(7) They must talk in any situation which, from their point of view, threatens their relationship with you. If you are angry or upset or weeping—no matter why—the child is apt to have more difficulty in talking.

Since these are some of the situations that result in increased non-fluency, it would seem wise to eliminate them in so far as that is possible. Certainly we will avoid deliberately creating such situations.

Suggestions for helping a child who has this problem of hesitations and repetitions begin on page 57.

4. What about older children who hesitate and repeat, are they stuttering?

Possibly. It all depends on how much hesitating and repeating they do, how they do it, and how they feel about it. As we have pointed out before, perfect fluency is out of the question for most of us. To be "a stutterer," the speaker must (1) have considerably more breaks in fluency (hesitations, repetitions, prolongations) than the average and (2) must experience some anxiety as a result of the non-fluency. The anxiety just referred to will exhibit itself in some type of "struggle behavior"—that is, the speaker will show tension in the facial muscles, he will squint his eyes, purse his mouth, or, with his mouth open, struggle to "get the sound out." What we see is not the stuttering, but the efforts of the speaker to overcome or avoid the stuttering. It is impossible to give a brief definition of stuttering from the stutterer's point of view, for there are involved not only non-fluency, and the grimaces and other struggle behavior, but also the stutterer's feelings about the non-fluency, his apprehensive anticipation of it and his reactions to it.

Suggestions for helping the child who stutters begin on page 60.

5. What causes stuttering?

The leading authorities in the field of speech pathology do not agree as to the exact cause of stuttering. During the more than thirty years since I took my first course in speech correction, much research has been completed. Many studies are now in progress. But there are still a number of questions about stuttering that have not been answered. Anything we have to say about the cause of this speech disorder must be tentative, subject to revision as more facts are determined.

In preceding paragraphs we pointed out that: (1) Most young children have hesitations and repetitions as a result of limitations of vocabulary and lack of skill in grammatical construction. (2) Children (and many adults, for that matter) find it more difficult to talk fluently in some situations than in others. Let's examine two more pieces of the puzzle, then we will try to fit them together.

The third piece of our puzzle involves the attitudes of the parents. Parents differ in many respects (no two of us are alike!). Let's look at some of the differences that may affect the child's speech. Some parents are more accepting and tolerant than others. Some are more critical and demanding. Some are "in a hurry" for their children to grow up, and are eager for them to do and say the things that are *exactly* right! Others, who love their children just as much, are content to let them mature more slowly and attach less importance to perfection (in either speech or behavior) . Some parents discover how to have courteous, pleasant children in a re-laxed, comfortable home atmosphere. Some believe that they must choose between "letting children run wild" or sternly "making them toe the line." Some parents maintain an orderly, comfortable, relaxed atmosphere in their homes. Some don't! You recall that in the majority of cases in which a young child is labeled "a stutterer" the label is first applied by the parents—not by a speech correction-ist. Apparently some parents are more sensitive to or more critical of non-fluency than others.

The fourth piece of our puzzle is the difference in children. Some seem to be made of much more durable "stuff" than others. Some seem to be "wound-tight" all the time, others seem to be quite placid. Some seem to be balanced on a needle point, and the least change in the emotional environment upsets them. Others seem to be balanced on a much wider base so that they weather the daily cross-currents of emotions with little difficulty. We know that some of the boys will be more "mechanically inclined" than others, and that some girls will become better cooks than others; it is probably true that some children will be more adept at speech than others—that is, some are "just naturally" more glib, some are "just naturally" less facile than others.

One of the interesting facts about this puzzle is that the pieces can be fitted together in several different ways—and the resulting pictures may be quite different.

Let's try to draw some conclusions. Most children go through a stage of non-fluency—of hesitating and repeating as they try to express themselves. If a child encounters many of the situations in which it is difficult to talk the non-fluency increases. If parents be-come anxious about the child's lack of fluency (perhaps labeling it "stuttering"), the child is apt to react to the anxiety of the parents. He reflects their tensions. His speech becomes more labored, less fluent. He tries hard to meet the standards set by the parents. He wants to please them by succeeding, but any situation that involves speech also involves the danger of failure. He doesn't want and may even fear your disapproval. In his efforts to avoid the "stuttering" (because it displeases you), he develops tensions that only make his speech less fluent. He may develop special anxieties or fear concerning certain "hard to say" sounds or words, or concerning specific situations. In his efforts to "get the word out" he may develop a wide variety of struggle behavior, such as pursing the lips, blinking the eyes, jerking the head, or clenching the fists. Repetition tends to "fix the pattern," and we have "a stutterer."

The story is told of a man who fell into a river; he could not swim and was being swept rapidly toward a dangerous waterfall. His friend ran along on the bank calling, "Don't worry! I'll get you out!" I don't know what happened to the man. I do know that much of our advice to the non-fluent child is just about as helpful as the friend on the bank. When we are tempted to say, "Slow down," or "Take a deep breath and start over," or "Think what you want to say, then tell me," remember the man on the river bank. These bits of advice may seem to bring temporary relief, but they don't get at the heart of the problem. In fact, they probably add to the anxiety the child already feels, for although we intend to be helpful, the child probably interprets such remarks as disapproval. We are, in effect, saying, "I don't like the way you talk." And if you don't like the way I talk, how can I be sure that you like *me?* Disapproval and anxiety may also be conveyed to the child by a slight scowl, a tensing of the muscles around the eyes, the set of the mouth, or even by the fixed smile we assume while we wait for him to finish his sentence. It is out of this tension, this self-consciousness about his speech, this feeling of failure or impending failure in talking that stuttering is created.

It is obvious, then, that it is not enough to say, "I try not to show any anxiety about his speech." You must not experience any anxiety. For the time being, this is the way he talks—and it's all right with us. He is our son. We love him. We let him know that we love him. We try to make him feel that he has a warm, comfortable, secure place in our affection and in his home.

Summed up briefly, we may say that stuttering in many cases seems to be a learned behavior pattern that develops out of a child's anxiety about his ability to speak satisfactorily; the anxiety is created by the reactions of others to his speech.

Although there are various theories about stuttering, there

is rather general agreement concerning what we can do about it where the young child is concerned. Let's look next at the ways in which we can help the child who has difficulties with fluency.

suggestions for helping a child who hesitates or repeats excessively

Most children have breaks in fluency—especially when they are frustrated, excited or frightened. Besides, they do not have the vocabulary or the command of language to express all of their thoughts and feelings. They are learning a complex method of communication and need help—not criticism. (If you have not already read the discussion of the questions in the section beginning on page 50, you should do so before you read the following.)

If you are still concerned about "stuttering," it would be wise to consult a qualified speech correctionist. Don't listen to neighbors, relatives, or anyone who is not professionally prepared in the field of speech pathology. They may have the best of intentions but their guessing probably isn't any better than yours. If the difficulty is in your thinking, your evaluation, your attitudes—the sooner you find out, the better. If the difficulty is in the child's speech, you will, of course, want to find out what you can do about it.

In the meantime, here are six "Don'ts" and nine "Do's" that usually help to solve the problem:

DON'T criticize or call attention to a child's non-fluent speech. If we say, "Stop and start over," "Think what you want to say before you start," or "Take a deep breath before you talk,"—these and similar statements may seem to work for a while, but actually they focus more attention on the speech, build up more tension, and increase the chances of the child developing into a stutterer.

DON'T feel sorry for the child or for yourself. For the time being, that is the way he talks, and, for the time being, that's all right. Be objective about it, and you will enjoy watching him acquire the vocabulary and the grammatical skills he needs.

DON'T decide that he must be right-handed. Consult a specialist, if you want to; otherwise, let the child decide this for himself. It won't hurt to say now and then, "Now roll the ball with the other hand," nor will it hurt to place his playthings so that it is easier for him to pick them up with the right hand. But if he insists upon using his left hand, it is probably wise to make no issue of it.

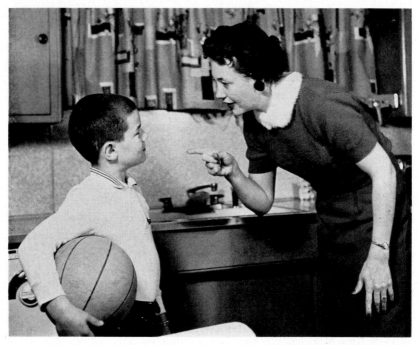

Figure 5: Wrong! Don't criticize or call attention to the child's hesitant speech.

DON'T criticize him for being awkard or clumsy. It may be that whatever causes him to be clumsy with his hands and feet is also causing him to be clumsy with his speech.

DON'T complain because he doesn't play well in a group. He wishes that he could and needs your help in learning how to get along with others.

DON'T try to force him to excel in other ways to make up for his inadequate or clumsy speech.

DO accept his speech just as it is. He will be aware of any tension or rejection on your part, and it will only add to his anxiety.

DO give attention to your child when he tries to tell you something. Most children, you remember, experience increased difficulty in talking when the listener is not paying attention or when they have to talk in competition with more fluent speakers. Let us be patient and understanding.

DO try to help your child develop the vocabulary he needs. Explanations and definitions should, of course, be simple enough for him to understand. Reading or telling stories to him, naming pictures in magazines and talking about them, going for walks and talking about what you see—these and similar activities will help.

DO provide as many pleasant and interesting experiences for your child as you can. Talk about them ahead of time. Let him help make the plans so that he knows his wishes are being considered. The more talking he does, the better.

DO bolster his confidence. Encourage him to try different activities and help him to discover things that he can do well.

DO make sure that your child is in the best possible health, that his hearing and vision are satisfactory.

Figure 6: Right! Provide as many pleasant experiences as possible, with opportunity to talk in a relaxed atmoshpere.

DO try to avoid the kind of situations or circumstances that make the symptoms more severe, and provide opportunities for him to talk in situations that minimize the symptoms.

DO let him know that you love him. A child needs the love and companionship of both parents. The sharing of activities or outings with father is particularly important. You know that you love him. Be sure he knows it.

DO make sure that he is not overshadowed by brothers or sisters. Each child must know that he is important to you. The child with some speech clumsiness is in special need of this assurance.

suggestions for helping a child who stutters

Therapy for stuttering must be highly individualized. It is impossible to describe in a few paragraphs or pages the varied approaches and diverse techniques that may be employed.

If the child is receiving help from a speech correctionist, it is imperative that the parents, teacher, and speech correctionist work closely together. Be sure to visit with the speech correctionist, follow the suggestions made, and see to it that assignments are carried out. With stuttering therapy, as with the correction of all other speech disorders, improvement is more rapid if regular practice periods are observed every day.

It is important to *encourage* the child to carry out the assignments that the speech correctionist makes, but it may be unwise to *demand* the performance. If difficulty is encountered, be sure to discuss it with the speech therapist.

Some of the assignments may not seem to "make any sense" to those who have not studied speech pathology. Try to accept, and help the child to accept, the fact that there is a reason back of every assignment and improvement will be more rapid if the daily assignments are carried out faithfully.

Sooner or later, the speech correctionist will try to teach your child ways of controlling his hesitations, repetitions, and/or grimaces. *You should make no effort toward controlling the child's speech* until the speech correctionist enlists your help. Then, encourage the child to follow the therapist's suggestions, but don't expect him to use the new technique all of the time, even though it seems to you that he talks "much better" while using it. At first, the child will have to concentrate on the control technique to such a degree that (from his point of view) it interferes with communication. As he uses the technique in regular practice periods, he becomes more adept at using it. As it becomes easier to use, he will, in all probability, begin to use it in more talking situations without any urging.

Remember, the stuttering is only the symptom that results from fears and anxieties. In many cases, once the fears and anxieties are modified or removed, the symptom tends to disappear.

You will want to keep in close touch with the speech correctionist to be sure that you are working together and not at cross-purposes.

What can I do to help when there is no speech correctionist?

In some cases, no speech thearpist is available. In that case, be sure to arrange through your school or public health nurse to have an interview with whatever diagnostic or consultation service is available.

There is much that the parents or the classroom teacher can do to help the young child who seems to be having more than his share of hesitations and interruptions, but who is not exhibiting anxiety or struggle behavior (see pages 53 and 54). However, therapy for a child who *really is stuttering* is a pretty complex affair. Dozens of books are devoted exclusively to the treatment of stuttering. It is impossible to learn all that you need to know from a booklet such as this. However, here are some suggestions that should help:

Read again the "Don'ts" and "Do's" on pages 57-60. With but slight modifications, these apply to children of all ages.

Help the child to the best possible personal and social adjustment. This suggestion does not imply that the child is at present maladjusted—some rather severe stutterers seem to be well-adjusted individuals. However, since stuttering interferes with communication, and communication is an important tool of adjustment, it is easy to understand why children with severe speech defects would find it more difficult to achieve good adjustment and, therefore, stand in need of a little more help.

As his adjustment improves, encourage him to do more talking. It is unwise to force him into situations where speech is required until he is ready for them. He will be ready when he feels that he is accepted and has developed self-assurance. If the child is emotionally upset by his speech, he should be required to do little or no talking, but center your attention on helping him toward a better adjustment.

A child who stutters should not be *forced* to read aloud or to recite. Opportunities should be provided, and he should be rewarded if he takes advantage of them. By creating an atmosphere of acceptance, we can do much toward helping the child find the desire and the courage to talk.

Get it out in the open! Children who are old enough to know that they are stuttering and are concerned or upset by it should be encouraged to talk about their speech problem and how they feel about it. (Remember, we are talking about a child who has been classified as a stutterer by a competent speech correctionist. We are *not* talking about the three to six year olds who are normally nonfluent.) If it is obvious that the child is concerned about his speech, an easy way for the teacher to introduce the subject is by inviting him to help work out decisions as to his participation in class. From there, he may be led to express his feelings of bewilderment, frustration, or concern. Later on, after he has learned that he can talk about his problem, he may be encouraged to talk to others in the class. Usually, when handled by a wise and sympathetic teacher, this results not only in much better understanding, but in improved relationships. CAUTION: If we are not certain that the child is "bothered" by his speech, we should not talk to him about it. Certainly we should not label the problem "stuttering." There is, however, much that can be done to help him without talking to him about it.

Provide experiences that will give the child a "feeling of success." This is especially important when the success involves speech. Most stutterers can talk with less difficulty in some situations than in others. Some can perform with little or no stuttering when they read, recite from memory, or play an impromptu role in which they are "not themselves." Sympathetic observation will help us discover the situations or circumstances in which he has the least difficulty. We can then arrange for him to do as much talking as possible in such situations. In other words, encourage the child to do as much as possible of the kind of talking he can do best. For a beginning with severe stutterers, try having the whole class recite in unison— such as in a verse speaking choir. (Examples: responsive reading in a ceremony, class yells, rituals for club meetings, poetry that may be read in unison, or boys read this portion, girls read this, etc.) The very young stutterer is particularly responsive to the effects of satisfying speaking experiences.

Help the child to discover his abilities in various fields and activities. If the problem of stuttering is severe, we tend to think of the child as "a stutterer," and lose sight of the many "normal" aspects or characteristics. The child himself tends to do this, too. By helping him discover and develop his interests and abilities, we help him to develop a better self-concept—that is, a good opinion of himself that is based on a realistic appraisal of his characteristics.

Help the child to form a wide circle of friends. Obviously, we can't just say, "Be friends!" But we can help in indirect ways. For one thing, we can encourage the child to participate in school activities: band, orchestra, chorus (I've never known a stutterer who had any trouble in singing), photography club, drama club— he can build scenery along with the best of them! The wider his circle of friends, the more he works and plays with other children, the better chance he has for good social adjustment, and the better chance we have for accomplishing some of the goals mentioned above. Another thing we can do is to express our attitudes of good will toward and appreciation of others. If we are critical and fault-finding, it is much harder to convince the child that people are friendly. If we express our appreciation of the good characteristics of others, it helps the child to see the good in others—and this is a step toward better social adjustment.

Help the child develop a love of learning. Many worthwhile hobbies are good avenues for learning, and some lead to vocations. The tactful suggestion of a good book, an informative or educational television program, an article about people and places that are in the news—all are helpful. The more the child learns, the wider his sphere of interests and information, the easier it is to develop into an interesting, stimulating adult.

Provide needed information. This goes beyond the suggestion made above. It includes information concerning good grooming, good manners or social graces, how to make introductions, what to say to your host, what to do on a date. Such information will not only help the child appear at his best, but will give him a feeling of competence or adequacy. He knows what to do or say, and can more comfortably enter various situations. In other words, help the child learn how to make the most of what he has to work with.

In some instances, the suggestions given above will be all that is necessary. In other cases, a speech problem may remain, but the child will be happier and more comfortable with it. Furthermore, a good foundation will have been laid for such time as professional help in the form of speech therapy may be available.

chapter v

voice problems

What causes a voice disorder?

Y OU REMEMBER THAT we described voice disorders as including problems of pitch (too high or too low), problems of quality (harsh, nasal, or otherwise unpleasant), problems of rate (too fast, too slow, or monotonous), and problems of flexibility of expression. With so many different problems included in this classification, any brief answer as to cause is bound to be both superficial and inadequate. However, some of the more common causes are:

Imitation. Many voice problems are the result of imitating poor speech models. Sometimes the model is a parent, an older sibling, or a favorite aunt or uncle. Sometimes a child consciously or unconsciously tries to sound like a beloved teacher.

Personality factors. Sometimes the voice problem reflects or is the result of an emotional problem. For example: the withdrawn child may talk with a lack of flexibility, that is, with little expression; the excessively shy child may talk with inadequate volume; the tensions felt by the anxious, insecure child may result in a harsh quality or a high pitch. In such cases, the voice problem is but a symptom. Before much permanent improvement can be expected, the emotional problem must be solved.

Adolescent voice change. During adolescence the boy's larynx or "voice box" increases in size very rapidly. The girl's larynx increases in size, too, but the change is not as great. For this reason, boys usually have more difficulty in controlling the pitch of the voice than do girls. Many boys learn to manage their "new" voices without much difficulty. For some, however, the problem is much more severe. Perhaps, for some reason, he experiences more embarrassing "breaks" in his voice; perhaps he is subjected to more cruel teasing; or perhaps he is more sensitive to the teasing and embarrassment. At any rate, some boys find this to be a traumatic experience.

Unsuitable pitch. A pitch that is not appropriate to the age and sex of the child is not only a problem in itself, it may cause a more serious problem. Appropriate pitch is necessary for adequate flexibility and loudness. Even more important, the continued use of an unsuitable pitch places the larynx under a strain, and the strain may cause a pathological condition (such as the development of nodules on the vocal folds). Sometimes the use of an unsuitable pitch is the result of parental pressure. They may want the boy to "sound like a man." Or the boy himself may try to imitate his favorite television hero and use a pitch that is unsuitable for his vocal mechanism.

Pathological conditions. Although pathological conditions that affect the voice of children are thought to be rare, they do exist. Sometimes a voice problem is the first indication that something is seriously wrong. The most common voice symptom connected with a serious throat condition is hoarseness. Whenever a child has a chronic hoarseness, the only safe procedure is to have him examined by a physician. If there is nothing wrong, we will be relieved; if there is something wrong, we can take whatever steps are necessary.

suggestions for helping a child who has a voice problem

With voice disorders, even more than with problems of articulation, it is desirable to have the parents, the teacher, and the professional speech correctionist work closely together. If your child is working with a speech correctionist, be sure to visit with him or her, and plan to observe your child during a speech lesson. The correctionist will make suggestions and give assignments which will need your cooperation.

As has been discussed briefly, there is a wide variety of voice problems. Therapy will differ, not only with the nature of the problem, but with the age of the child. Although the importance of consulting a speech correctionist cannot be overemphasized, there are some things that you can do even when no professional help is available.

A detailed therapeutic program cannot be presented in this short space, but some general suggestions will be helpful.

Be sure that the child is in good health and that he gets plenty of rest and a well-balanced diet.

Make the child's environment as pleasant and as calm as possible. (See the suggestions for helping stutterers on pages 61-64. These are, for the most part, suggestions that will be helpful to all children.)

Be sure to set a good speech model for the child to imitate. Use your own "best" voice.

Encourage the child to imitate a variety of voices. If he is able to imitate "better" voices, encourage him to do more of this type of imitation. Be sure, however, that you do not urge him to use a pitch that is too high or too low for his own vocal mechanism. He may try to change in order to please you, but the speech mechanism won't. (See "Unsuitable pitch" on page 66.)

Help the child to "hear the difference" between the voice he habitually uses and the "voice he can imitate." He must know what he is working for. He must be able to hear the difference. He must believe that the goal is worth the work it takes to reach it.

When he is imitating other voices, give them names: "the talking-through-your-nose voice," "the growling-dog voice," "the squeaky-hinge voice," "the talking-to-yourself voice," "the handsome-prince voice," or "the brave-cowboy voice." Such names will help the child discriminate between good and bad quality or pitch, as well as desirable and undesirable levels of loudness. Care must be taken not to use names or descriptive terms that will add to the child's anxiety or self-consciousness.

Even when the child is able to produce a voice of good quality, we cannot expect him to use it consistently. Insistense upon the desired voice production should be limited to a brief "good speech period" once or twice a day. The problem should be ignored the rest of the time.

If the child resents your efforts to help (in spite of your efforts to keep the "speech lesson" lighthearted and casual) , if he shows increased tensions or anxieties, it is probably wise to postpone any effort to help him until you can work under the direction of a professional speech correctionist.

If the voice problem becomes more severe, be sure to see a

throat specialist. This is necessary in order to "play safe" with the child's health.

As was stated earlier, therapy for voice disorders is determined by the exact nature of the problem. In this area of difficulty, even more than with problems of articulation, it is important that the parent or teacher who is attempting therapy consult with a speech correctionist before beginning to work with the child. Certainly a speech correctionist should be consulted before going beyond the seven suggestions given above.

PART II

hearing problems

chapter vi

some questions and answers about hearing loss

1. What is meant by "hard of hearing"?

A PERSON WHO IS "hard of hearing" is one who has a hearing loss, but even with this loss is able to learn speech in the normal manner—that is, "by ear." The speech may be imperfect, for if he cannot hear speech perfectly he cannot reproduce it perfectly. With lip-reading (often called "speech reading"), and with some form of amplification (such as an individual hearing aid that he wears, or a desk-type hearing aid) the hard-of-hearing person is able to communicate adequately. The help of a speech correctionist may be needed to help him improve his speech.

2. What is meant by "deaf" or "deafened"?

A person who is deaf has a more severe hearing loss than one who is referred to as "hard-of-hearing." He may be able to hear some loud sounds, but he does not have enough hearing to serve the purposes of communication even with the help of a hearing aid. A child who is deaf will not learn speech in the normal way—he cannot hear enough of it. Highly specialized techniques must be used to teach him speech. It is a slow process, and the work of a well-prepared teacher will be required. However, there is a great deal that informed parents can do to help such a child. (Suggestions are offered in another chapter.)

If a person becomes deaf after he has acquired speech, he is called "deafened." His problems are not the same as those of a person who is born deaf. The deafened person will, of course, be able to use speech to express himself, but will not be able to understand speech (even with a hearing aid) unless he is taught to read lips. Since he cannot hear his own speech, it tends to deteriorate. A speech correctionist may be needed to help a deafened person maintain his good speech patterns.

3. Could a child be hard-of-hearing and neither parents nor teachers be aware of it?

Yes! Surprising as it may seem, many children are handicapped by a loss of hearing without anyone suspecting it. It is possible for a child to have a type of hearing loss that lets him hear speech and other sounds, only they are fainter to him than to a person of normal hearing. A child with this kind of hearing loss would not hear the soft spoken, "Johnny, please don't do that," so he does it! Then we descend upon him shouting, "I told you to stop that!" And he hears that, because it was loud enough. A teacher said of such a child, "He's not stupid. He's just lazy and doesn't pay attention. If I have him sit close to me and talk right to him, he will do his work. He needs discipline." A mother said, "He's stubborn. He won't pay any attention unless I get angry and yell at him." Both of these criticisms were unfair. When the sound was loud enough for the child to hear, he responded.

A little harder to understand is a "regional hearing loss." With this kind of loss, a person can hear some sounds as well as anyone with normal hearing but has trouble hearing other sounds. In relation to learning speech, a person with a regional loss might hear all of the vowel sounds, but be unable to hear consonant sounds. When we quietly say, "Dickie!" he looks up and comes to us—so we feel confident that he hears. But he didn't hear all we said. He heard only the vowels. If we say, "Dickie, put the cat out," it sounds to him like, "I-ee, u uh a ou." He may learn to understand and respond to what he hears, but without special help, he will not learn to talk correctly. How could he? He doesn't hear the consonant sounds so he can't be expected to learn them and use them. Furthermore, he will often misunderstand what is said. He may profit from the use of a hearing aid; certainly he should have lessons in lip-reading.

Frequently, a "regional loss' is not detected until parents become concerned about the child's poor speech.

4. What are the indications of a hearing loss?

Children with hearing defects may show one or more of the following symptoms:

a. Inability to locate the direction from which a sound is coming.

b. More than normal use of hands in making wants known.

c. A voice that lacks an intonation pattern and resonance. (It's monotonous, unpleasant.)

d. A voice that is too loud or not loud enough. (Sometimes the child who sounds like a "bully" or the child who seems to be "very shy—afraid of his own voice," actually has a hearing loss.) While it may sound contradictory, it is a fact that a hearing loss may lead to either excessively loud or very soft speech, depending largely upon the nature of the loss.

e. Faulty equilibrium. He finds it difficult to keep his balance, particularly in the dark or when blindfolded for a game.

f. Speech defects. If a child hears speech imperfectly, he will speak incorrectly.

g. Lack of attention. The strain of trying to hear and understand is very tiring for a hard-of-hearing child. Like most of us, they reach a point where they stop trying to "pay attention."

h. Frequent mistakes in carrying out directions. "Watch the baby" may be understood as "Wash the baby."

i. Irrelevant answers. (He answered the question as he understood it!)

j. Turning of the head to catch the sound with the better ear; peculiar listening posture.

k. Anxious or listless expression, depending on the temperament of the child.

l. Repeated earaches.

m. Ear discharge.

n. Requests for repetition of what has been said.

o. Complaint of head noises.

p. Restlessness and evidence of nervous fatigue.

q. Persistent truancy or other forms of unusual behavior due to failure in making a good educational or social adjustment.

5. Could an infant be deaf and parents not be aware of it?

Total deafness in an infant is very seldom found. Even though he does not have enough hearing to learn speech "by ear" as most children do, and so is classified as "deaf," he may have enough hearing to respond to loud sounds. He may hear the slamming of a door, the ringing of the telephone, or even the louder vowel sounds of speech so that he reacts to these sounds much as an infant with normal hearing does. Even those who have very little hearing may respond to the vibrations of a door slamming, heavy footsteps, or a plane flying overhead.

In Chapter II we discussed the various stages of the acquisition of speech. The deaf baby may laugh and cry quite normally. Since babbling is spontaneous, the result of random activity (much like the continuous waving of arms and legs), the deaf baby babbles, just as other children do. He gurgles and coos and smiles—and we have no reason to suspect a hearing loss.

Sometimes a deaf infant may be so alert, so responsive to facial expressions that he seems to be responding to speech. Many a deaf child develops some skill in lip-reading—enough to enable him to respond appropriately. But as he grows older and communication becomes more complicated, he is unable to interpret the rapid movements of the lips. Then, too, when he begins to crawl and we speak to him from such a distance that he does not see our lips, and does not respond, then we begin to worry.

Because he "seemed to hear" parents sometimes make the mistake of labeling the child "stubborn," "naughty," "unresponsive," or even "stupid," when, as a matter of fact, he just doesn't hear well enough to understand what is required of him.

6. How can I tell if my infant is deaf?

There are several tests that you can make that will determine whether or not your child is deaf. Unfortunately, you will not be able to prove that he has normal hearing. The surest way to determine the presence of normal hearing or the precise extent of a loss is with an audiometric test administered by a qualified audiologist. But long before a child is old enough to give reliable responses to such formal testing, you can either satisfy yourself that he is not deaf, or convince yourself that he has enough of a hearing loss to warrant seeking professional advice at once!

(1) If, when he is sleeping, noises do not rouse him, but he wakens at a touch or a slight jar (such as the bumping of his crib), you may have reason to suspect a hearing loss. Of course children

Figure 7: Simple tests of an infant's hearing may be administered by the parents. By the age of four months a child who hears may be expected to try to locate the source of a sound.

sleep more soundly at some times than at others, so one incident is not enough to be particularly disturbing.

(2) By the time he is two months old the infant should react to a sudden loud noise by jerking his arms and legs, blinking, or

crying. Banging pan lids, blowing a shrill whistle, or crumpling of paper close to the baby's ear should produce a startled response. You will want to be sure that your noise-making does not produce a vibration or a puff of air that he might feel.

(3) Try holding a music box with a pretty tune close to his ear. For a moment or two, while he gives attention to the new sensation, he should be relatively quiet. However, you should not expect him to listen for more than a few moments, for his attention span is too short.

(4) About the age of four months he may be expected to show an interest in locating the source of sounds. If he reaches, kicks, and gurgles when a pretty rattle is held in front of him, we can expect him to give some indication of hearing and searching for the sound if the same rattle is sounded behind him. Just be sure that he can not see any movement or shadow.

(5) In general, a baby may be expected to show growing interest in sounds as his interest in objects that he can see increases. If he continues to be more aware of movement and objects than he is of sounds, there may be some cause for concern.

If he passes these informal tests, you may be assured that he is not deaf, although there may be some hearing loss. If he fails consistently, it would be wise to consult your pediatrician or an ear specialist.

7. *What should be done if a child has symptoms of a hearing loss?*

The symptoms of a hearing loss listed above are only indicative, but they are important enough to warrant further investigation. The same may be said of the "tests of hearing" that may be administered at home to the infant. Only the skilled audiologist or otologist can determine whether the child's hearing is normal or impaired.

If the child about whom you are concerned is in school, he should be referred through the school for a hearing test. If your area is served by a speech correctionist, he or she may test the child. In some communities the public health nurse is prepared to do audiometric testing. Your school and health department should know what facilities are available for an evaluation of your child's hearing and help you make an appointment. Without audiometric testing we can only guess at the extent of the problem. If a hearing loss is found, the child should be seen by an otologist or ear-specialist for further examination.

If the child involved is an infant, the problem is a little more difficult, for audiometric testing requires the co-operation of the person being tested. However, an audiologist or an otologist will be able to determine whether or not a severe loss is present even in an infant. If the audiologist finds a loss, he will recommend that you take your child to an otologist.

8. What is the difference between an audiologist and an otologist?

An otologist is a doctor of medicine who has specialized in diseases of the ear. Some otologists do more "testing of hearing" than others, but their primary concern is with the medical and surgical treatment of hearing problems; that is, they determine the cause of the hearing loss and try to correct it.

An audiologist is concerned with the measurement of the exact extent of the hearing loss, the interpretation of the effect of the loss in terms of communication and education, and the habilitation of the child (or the rehabilitation of the adult) . He may recommend instruction in lip-reading, speech therapy, auditory training, the use of a hearing aid, enrollment in a special class, or whatever in his expert opinion is needed for the best interests of the person concerned.

The findings of the audiologist often help the otologist in his diagnosis of the hearing problem. On the other hand, the diagnosis of the otologist guides the audiologist in making his recommendations.

9. What good will an otological examination do if the child cannot hear?

Sometimes hearing can be improved by proper treatment. In other cases, steps can be taken to keep the loss from getting any greater. In still other cases, proper treatment is needed to keep an infection of the ear from spreading to the brain where it would do serious (even fatal) damage. Only an otologist can determine whether the loss will be progressive and what medical or surgical steps should be taken, if any.

Furthermore, an ear specialist's diagnosis is often needed by the audiologist to help determine whether the provision of a hearing aid or lip-reading instruction is desirable.

Figure 8: When in doubt about your child's hearing consult an audiologist or an otologist. This boy is receiving an audiometric test to determine just how well he hears.

10. If instruction in lip-reading is recommended, how can it be obtained?

If your area is served by a speech correctionist, it may be possible to include your child in the schedule. Speech correctionists know how to teach speech-reading or lip-reading; however, your cooperation in the program will be essential.

If your school district does not have a speech correctionist, write to your state's Bureau for Handicapped Children or to the Director of Special Education, Department of Public Instruction for information concerning the best way for your child to secure this instruction. There may be a facility near you, or there may be a state-supported summer program.

Whether the child is in school or too young to be in school, there is a great deal that can be done to help the child who has a hearing loss whether he be deaf or hard-of-hearing.

11. If no instruction in lip-reading is available, what can I do?

Suggestions for helping the child who is hard-of-hearing are to be found in Chapter VIII. Suggestions for helping the child who is deaf are offered in Chapter IX.

12. What causes a hearing loss?

The answers to this and related questions are found in the following chapter which deals with the ear and how it functions.

13. When is enrollment in a special class desirable?

In general, it is better for a child with a mild to moderate hearing loss to continue in the regular classroom. With the understanding of the teacher, the encouragement of the parents, and the assistance of a hearing aid and lip-reading, hard-of-hearing children usually make a satisfactory adjustment to the regular classroom. Sometimes it is helpful for them to leave the regular classroom for short periods to receive lessons in speech or in lip-reading (or both). In some schools, a hard-of-hearing child leaves the regular classroom for special help in academic areas that are difficult for him because of his hearing loss. Sometimes the parents must anticipate the difficulties and provide this extra help at home. We must remember, however, that even though a hearing aid may give the child nearly normal hearing, it does not "fill in all of the gaps" in his learning that resulted from the years spent with impaired hearing. It will take time and help for him to "catch up."

If the hearing loss is so severe that the child, even with a hearing aid and speech-reading, cannot make satisfactory progress in the regular classroom, special class or special school enrollment should be considered. In fairness to the child we must provide all of the help that especially prepared teachers can provide.

Figure 9: Many hard of hearing children can, with the help of lip-reading lessons and hearing aids, make a satisfactory adjustment to the regular classroom. Two of the children in this class are using desk-type portable amplifiers; the boy standing is using a "wearable" hearing aid.

14. Should a deaf child wear a hearing aid?

That depends upon several factors. Remember, a child may not have enough hearing to learn speech "by ear" in the normal manner (and so be classified as deaf) , and still have considerable hearing. Many deaf children get enough sound from a hearing aid to help them in several ways: it may enable them to hear warning sounds—bells, sirens, automobile horns; it may help them to know at least that sound is present; it may enable them to get the rhythm and emphasis of speech.

Your audiologist will be able to advise you on this question. However, with very young children, one test is to introduce music through a hearing aid. If he gives evidence of hearing it and particularly if he shows any interest in it, you have a good indication that he will profit from wearing a hearing aid.

Frequently a trial period of several months is required to determine just how much benefit a child will derive from a hearing aid. During this time he should be introduced to the aid for short periods each day. Efforts should be made to make this a pleasant and interesting experience.

We must remember that sounds will not be meaningful to him the first time he hears them. The hearing child has been "bathed in sound"—your voice in speech and song, the television, the radio, the record player—and has developed many associations that give meaning to sound. Not so with the deaf child! The first time that he hears sounds amplified through the hearing aid may be the first sounds that he hears. They will be strange. They may even seem unpleasant. The audiologist or the teacher of the deaf can guide you in introducing the hearing aid. It should not be put on the child without professional guidance!

Most hearing aid manufacturers belong to an association that is constantly striving to raise the standards of service that their sales representatives provide. Their salesmen are being given more and more training in how to help the hard-of-hearing person. But as this is written, hearing aid manufacturers are not even claiming to have salesmen who are trained to guide you in introducing your child to a hearing aid. This is a highly specialized field. Because the first experience with amplified sound is tremendously important in determining whether your child will *want* to hear, it is important that you have the best advice possible. In fact, if you have not secured the advice of a qualified teacher of the deaf, an audiologist, or a certified speech correctionist who has had preparation in the area of hearing rehabilitation it may be wise to postpone placing a hearing aid on a deaf child until such advice is obtained.

On the other hand, with proper guidance, you may begin to let a child as young as eighteen months hear amplified sound. The use of the hearing aid by an infant must, of course, be under your strict supervision. But the sooner we start using whatever hearing the child has, the sooner he becomes aware of the world of sound (even though he hears it imperfectly), the better are his chances of acquiring the communication skills we want him to have.

15. Will a hearing aid ruin what hearing he has?

Parents are sometimes told by well-meaning neighbors, "I wouldn't let my child wear a hearing aid. Why, he never will learn

Figure 10: Very young children may profit from the use of a hearing aid under adult supervision. This little girl, just getting acquainted with her aid, is hearing the jingle of bells for the first time.

to hear if you give him that crutch to lean on." There is no evidence to the effect that using a hearing aid will decrease the child's ability to hear. Not many hearing aids are capable of producing enough sound to damage the hearing apparatus, and before any damage is done the child will complain of discomfort. I don't know how this "old wives' tale" originated, but there is no basis for it. The evidence at hand indicates that we should provide the best possible hearing. If a qualified person recommended the use of a hearing aid—even on an experimental basis to determine how much it will help—I'd certainly want a child of mine to have that advantage.

16. Will a hearing aid enable a child with a hearing loss to learn to speak normally?

If the hearing loss is such that a hearing aid will enable the child to hear all of the sounds of speech, he may in time learn to talk correctly. But we must not expect him to start talking as soon as the aid is put on him. Just as the child with normal hearing spends many months being "immersed in sound" before he understands much of what he hears, more months before he begins to talk, and still more months before he acquires the articulatory skill and the vocabulary to express himself adequately—so the child who, through the acquisition of a hearing aid, begins to hear speech will require months of stimulation and effort. Usually, some speech therapy is needed to help correct faulty speech patterns that he has acquired.

Sometimes progress is so slow that parents are not aware of it and become discouraged, even though an articulation test shows that the child's speech is improving. It may help parents to avoid discouragement if they keep a notebook in which they enter a record of the child's accomplishments. For example, "Billy said 'baw' today when he wanted his ball, until today he just said 'aw'." Or later, "Billy said 'kitten' today instead of 'titten." Or, "Aunt Jane hadn't seen Billy for six weeks. Today she said that she could notice a big improvement in his speech." Looking back over such a notebook may be a source of encouragement. But remember, progress will probably be slow. It is even for the child with normal hearing.

If the child has a more severe hearing loss, the use of a hearing aid will not be enough. He will need help in learning to read lips and to produce sounds that he doesn't hear. But even if the hearing aid does no more than enable him to get the rhythm and possibly the inflections of normal speech, that will be a tremendous help to him. It may make the difference between the laborious production of the sounds: *Mike un tree,* which is meaningless, and the rhythmical production of the same sounds which result in the familiar "My country."

With perceptive type hearing loss (damage to the inner ear or the nerve) a hearing aid may enable a child to hear, but not necessarily to distinguish speech sounds. You have been in an auditorium listening to a speaker when something went wrong with the public address system. The speech seemed loud enough, but it was garbled, indistinct, and making it louder didn't help. That's about the effect you get with some types of hearing loss. Of course it's a big help for the child to hear the patterns of speech. He knows that someone is talking, he gets the rhythm and the inflections of speech, and that will make it easier for him to learn to talk intelligibly (even though he must rely on lip-reading in order to understand what is said), but of course he will need speech therapy.

17. Will he ever learn to read lips if I let him use a hearing aid?

If the child is deaf, he will not get enough help from a hearing aid to enable him to learn speech "by ear." In order to understand you it will be necessary for him to supplement what he hears with what he sees. The hearing aid may be of great help, but it will encourage rather than discourage his lip-reading.

In cases of progressive hearing loss—when we know that the loss will gradually become greater—we much prefer to start lessons in speech-reading before that skill is really needed for communication. It is much easier to teach lip-reading to someone who has enough hearing to enable him to "piece together" what he sees with what he hears.

If a qualified audiologist or otologist recommends a hearing aid, you may confidently let your child use one.

18. Should I insist that he use the hearing aid?

It is probably unwise to *insist* that a child wear his hearing aid. Children need to be introduced to the hearing aid for brief "get acquainted" periods, and we should try to make those periods interesting and pleasant. But the child will not want to use it for long at a time. When he loses interest—that's enough. Try it again for a short period later in the day.

Often a child of school age quickly recognizes the benefits of wearing an aid, but children vary a great deal in the way that they accept a hearing aid. Some children seem to be fascinated by it. They quickly reach the point where they put it on in the morning when they dress, as casually as they put on their shoes. Larry, for example, seemed to enjoy his aid and the sounds it brought to him from the very first. Deborah, a six-year-old, is just beginning to wear hers. She has had it for nearly a year. During that time she played with it, put it on her doll, had her mother wear it, and even took it to bed with her. She took it to a motion picture theater, and in the darkness of the theater her mother observed that she inserted the ear piece. Why didn't she want to wear it? She can't tell you. But her parents were patient—and at last she is beginning to wear the aid for short periods.

The happy, well-adjusted child will gradually develop longer periods of interest. The time will come when he will not need your supervision in using the aid. Many preschool children care for their own aids—insert the ear piece, adjust the volume, dependably turn off the switch when they take it off, and even change batteries.

Don't be surprised if older children want to take off (or turn off) their hearing aids at times—just as many of us who wear glasses like to take them off, but we gladly put them back on when there is something we want to see—and the child will turn his aid back on when there is something that he wants to hear. (I know one five-year-old who surreptitiously turns off his aid whenever he is being scolded!) Obviously, if listening experiences are pleasant and interesting the child will more quickly become adjusted to wearing the aid all of the time.

During the "get acquainted" period, if the child gives evidence that the amplified sound is causing pain or discomfort, turn down the volume. If he still complains, don't insist that he use the aid, but consult your "advisor" at the first opportunity.

19. Should I talk to him?

Sometimes parents say, "I feel silly talking to him when I know he can't hear me." Nevertheless, the more talk the better. And you shouldn't feel silly about it. Parents talk to children who have normal hearing long before the children can understand the words they use. That's an important part of stimulating their interest in language and communication. In fact, if no one talked to the child, he would never learn to talk! It's much the same with the deaf or hard-of-hearing child. The chief difference is that such a child will need to rely on what he sees, rather than what he hears. To be more accurate, the deaf child must rely on what he sees supplemented by what he hears—for remember, few children are born with no hearing at all. Talk to him just as you did (or would) to a child with normal hearing. Sing to him as you hold him. Talk to him as you bathe him. We will have more to say about this later, for talking to the infant is absolutely necessary.

20. Will he understand me?

Does a hearing infant understand what is said to him? Of course not. Not at first. But he understands your loving care! Gradually he begins to understand the situation. Then he recognizes a few key words. For example, he may recognize the word "ball" in a sentence. If he has the ball, he gives it to you. If he doesn't have it, he goes to look for it. If you have it, he reaches for it. Later he will get more meaning from the other words of the sentence and will rely less on the situation. It's much the same with the deaf child— only he must recognize the words by the movement of the lips. That's more difficult and takes longer. But most children acquire this skill in varying degrees. We'll offer some suggestions later for helping a child to learn lip-reading.

21. Will he learn to talk?

Hard-of-hearing children are usually able to acquire satisfactory speech, although they may need a little more time and a little more help than the child with normal hearing.

Many deaf children learn to talk well enough to communicate with their families and intimate friends. Some (with adequate training) learn to talk well enough to be easily understood by strangers. Some do not learn to talk at all. What your child achieves in communicative skills depends to an impressive degree upon the help that you give him during his pre-school years. In addition to reading the suggestions given in Chapter IX, you will want to seek the guidance of the best qualified person available.

But remember two things: first, neither the deaf child's ability to speak nor his ability to read lips is directly related to his intelligence—no more than a hearing child's ability to play the violin! Second, speech is only one form of communication. It's convenient, and it's conventional (at least for hearing persons) —but it isn't the only way. In fact, some people refer to the sign-language as "the mother tongue of the deaf." It may not lend itself to delicate shades of meaning, but it is rapid and direct. Every child should be given the opportunity to learn to express himself orally. The deaf child should have the help of his parents and the instruction of skilled teachers. But if, after several years of instruction "by experts" he is not mastering this difficult skill, let's not worry about it. The responsibility for communication rests upon those who have normal hearing! It is much easier for a hearing person to learn the sign-language than it is for a deaf person to learn to speak. Why shouldn't we learn the sign-language? Let me repeat: oral communication has many advantages, and every deaf child should have the opportunity to learn to speak, but if he cannot, how in good conscience can we refuse to learn his language?

22. *Should I try to teach him?*

Yes, indeed! Not in formal lessons or drills. Not grimly and insistently. No matter how conscious we are of his need to learn to speak and to read lips, we must "make haste slowly." If we are tense and anxious, if we try to force the child to watch our lips, if we insist upon formal "teaching" we are sure to fail. Rather, our teaching must occur during the interesting experiences of everyday living. "Use language that lives" and "live language with the child" are expressions used by writers in this field to stress the importance of teaching language (not just words) in meaningful, happy situations.

Suggestions for helping your child learn to read lips and for helping him learn to talk are offered in later sections. These suggestions should "get you off on the right foot," but you should seek professional guidance at the first opportunity.

23. *Where can I get professional guidance?*

The otologist or ear specialist who determined that your child has a hearing problem, the public health nurse, and your local school authorities should all know the nearest place for you to secure the advice and guidance of a person professionally prepared to teach young deaf or hard-of-hearing children. There may be a nursery school for deaf children in your own or a nearby community. Many speech correctionists have had some preparation in this area of special education. Perhaps there are special classes or a special school for the deaf not too far from you. A nearby college may have a clinic or a special education center where you may get advice. Don't accept the first "There's no one available" as final. If you can't get the information locally, write to the Bureau for Handicapped Children or the Department of Special Education, in care of your State Department of Public Instruction.

Whether or not local help is available, you will find the Volta Bureau, 1537 35th Street N. W., Washington 7, D. C., an excellent source of information. It was founded by Alexander Graham Bell in 1887 and has an enormous library on hearing problems. You may borrow books free of charge, or purchase helpful leaflets and books at nominal cost.

If there is no experienced teacher of deaf children to guide you, the next best thing is a correspondence course. Probably the best known course of this kind is that furnished free of charge by the John Tracy Clinic. No correspondence course can take the place of personal conferences, but the fact that more than 11,000 families from all 50 states and 64 foreign countries have been enrolled in the program is evidence of its helpfulness. Furthermore, the course has been translated into nine foreign languages, and permission has been granted for translation into seven others.

The course is designed for children between the ages of two and six years. However, there is special material for use with even younger children, and the course may be adapted to use with children who are older. There are twelve lessons or installments that cover a wide variety of topics including language, activities, attitudes, and teaching materials. At the end of each lesson there is a questionnaire which parents must complete and return before the next installment is sent. Along with the next lesson, parents receive a personal letter that seeks to answer the questions they raised, give suggestions for dealing with problems that have been encountered, and suggest ways of adapting lessons to the needs of the particular child. These personal letters are an important part of the help that is provided.

To enroll in the course, parents need only write to the John Tracy Clinic, 806 West Adams Boulevard, Los Angeles 7, California. There is no charge for the course, but any contribution you may wish to make will be used to further the work of the clinic.

The John Tracy Clinic and a number of colleges and universities have summer programs for deaf children and their parents. You may write to your State Department of Public Instruction or your State Department of Public Health for information concerning a program near you.

24. If he can't hear me, is it "right" to discipline him?

Over-protection and over-indulgence are no better for the deaf or hard-of-hearing child than they are for the child with normal hearing. If we "just can't bear to discipline the dear child because he's deaf," we may be avoiding difficulties for the moment, but we are creating future difficulties for the family and inevitable problems for the child. Unless we want a child who is unreasonable, "spoiled," and unhappy, we must teach him to respect the rights and property of others, and to obey limits that are set for his own safety—and this involves discipline.

There are three important guideposts for disciplining a child with a severe hearing loss: consistency, reasonableness, and patience. Let's take a look at them.

(1) *Be consistent.* Of course consistency is important in the disciplining of all children, but it is imperative in dealing with the child who has a hearing problem. Lack of consistency confuses him

as to what is expected of him. Yesterday he spilled your powder all over himself, and you laughed, hugged him, and perhaps took his picture. Today he got spanked for the same behavior. From his point of view, your behavior must seem unreasonable and unpredictable. Will he be hugged or spanked if he does it again?

Having set limits, we must consistently enforce them. Recently I was in a home when a child "threw a temper tantrum." When order was finally restored the mother said, "This has been going on for two weeks—almost every time I say 'no.' It started when we had company. It was past Sally's bedtime, and she cried when I said, 'No.' To keep her quiet, I gave in. I'm sorry I did. I just wonder how long it will take me to teach her that when I say 'no' I mean it, and a temper tantrum won't do any good." Such is the price of inconsistency!

(2) *Be reasonable.* If we refrain from acting too hastily, it will help us to be consistent without being inflexible. If we are not in such a hurry to say, "No, you can't" or "Oh yes you will!" we will find ourselves less often in the awkward position of having to reverse our original decision or suffer the uncomfortable feeling that we have been unfair to the child for the sake of consistency.

To a hearing child we can explain the reasons for our reversal. But it is often impossible to explain to the deaf child.

Most of us have punished children unjustly at some time or other. Perhaps we were frightened or angry and punished the child for some incident we would otherwise have ignored. Perhaps, in thinking it over, we realized that the child's apparent "misbehavior" was the result of our inadequate explanations. Perhaps we discovered that, at the time we punished the child, we had not been aware of all of the facts in the case. To the hearing we can say, "I'm sorry I spanked you. I know now that you didn't mean to be naughty. I should have given you a chance to explain. I'm sorry, and I apologize." The youngster will probably answer, "That's all right, daddy. I'm not mad at you any more."

But if daddy's apology is not heard, his attempts to "make-up" for the unjust punishment by being extra friendly and affectionate may arouse suspicion and anxiety. The youngster may think, "This is the 'giant' who hurt me last night for no reason. What's he up to now? Can I trust him?"

It is always important to be reasonable in dealing with children. With deaf children, reasonableness is imperative.

(3) *Be patient.* Remember, it isn't his fault that he can't hear. It probably isn't your fault, either, but you are the adults and it is your responsibility to help him develop into the happy, self-sufficient individual you want him to be. No matter how "bright" he is, the fact that he cannot hear is a barrier to communication, and some difficult situations will be sure to arise.

Let's visit the home of Marjorie and David. Marjorie is three years old and deaf. David is seven and has normal hearing. Marjorie starts for David's model airplane. She doesn't hear David say, "Mother, make Marjorie stop!" Nor does she hear mother say, "No, no, Marjorie. That's David's." She has no warning of impending crisis until, in a storm of scowls and angry movements, David roughly spins her around and snatches the airplane from her. David is older, faster, and stronger—and usually succeeds in rescuing his prized possessions. What does Marjorie learn? Only that if she wants something she must grab faster and hold on tighter. When this doesn't work, there's nothing left for Marjorie to do but cry with frustration. Before long, she responds by crying whenever anyone starts toward her—she has learned that they are probably going to take away whatever she is playing with.

Let's view the same situation again. Marjorie starts for the model airplane. David hurries across the room, snatching up his prettiest ball on the way. He takes the airplane from Marjorie and says, "This is an airplane, a model airplane. I am making it. I'm not finished yet. You can't play with it because it would break. Here is the ball you like, you play with it." Now, Marjorie has understood little if anything of what David said, but she has had a good look at the airplane, and she knows that she has been treated with respect. (The real David in this story went further—he sat down on the floor and played at rolling the ball to Marjorie.)

It may help us to be patient if we remember that for the child who is deaf, sight and touch must take the place of hearing. It is unfortunate that we can't send to the corner store for an extra supply of patience and ingenuity, for we will need both in helping the deaf child overcome his difficulty in communication.

The deaf child will need help to understand many situations

that the hearing child will grasp readily. When mother is called to the telephone in the midst of some interesting activity, the hearing child may not understand the casual statement, "I have to answer the telephone. I'll be back." But he recognizes some connection between the ringing of the bell and mother's departure. The deaf child has quite a different experience. He is enjoying mother's attention, then suddenly she hurries away! In his frustration and anxiety he may cry. This annoys mother who is at the telephone. She's "at her wits end" and that doesn't help the situation any when she returns to the crying child. It would be helpful if this mother had followed the example of Marjorie's mother. When the telephone rang, she picked up Marjorie and hurried to the telephone, she put Marjorie's fingers on the 'phone so that she could feel the vibration, then Marjorie watched while her mother picked up the receiver and talked. Part of the time Marjorie's fingers were held between the earpiece and mother's ear, so that she could feel more vibrations. Instead of being abruptly deserted, she shared with mother an interesting experience.

Consistency, reasonableness, and patience! These must temper our discipline. Some days will go more smoothly than others. The reason for this probably lies as much with variations of mood, health, and emotional state of the parents as of the child. But in any home with normal, growing children there are times when toys are strewn all over the floor, when one or more children are crying, and it seems that bedtime can't come soon enough. This being the case, we will not expect any method of dealing with the deaf child to produce a completely and continuously tranquil atmosphere. However, a thick serving of reasonableness between slices of consistency and patience will work wonders—not only in matters of discipline, but in helping the child mature into a happy adult.

25. Should I go to another doctor?

Where anything as important as your child's hearing is concerned you will, of course, want the best advice available. It is extremely difficult if not impossible to get a precise measurement of a young child's hearing. So many things can influence a child's reactions in the clinic or doctor's office, that it is often necessary to see a child more than once to reach a conclusion in regard to his hearing ability. However, a competent audiologist or otologist who is accustomed to working with children can usually be pretty sure whether or not a severe loss is present.

If you wish, go to someone else for a second evaluation. But don't spend a lot of time and money "shopping" for a doctor who will tell you what you would like to hear. It would be wiser, especially with infants, to accept the opinion that your child is deaf, and give him as much help as possible. When he is a little older, it will be easier to get reliable results from testing. You may then find that he has more—or less—hearing than was at first suspected. But give him the benefit of all of the help that you can provide in the meantime. If it turns out that he is not deaf, you have not hurt him in any way. If he is deaf, you are off to a good start on his education.

26. Will the doctor want me to put my deaf infant in a school for the deaf?

No! Most residential schools for the deaf will not accept infants. Babies need the love and understanding that only parents can give. During the early years the parents can do some very important things toward helping the child become a happy, well-adjusted, self-confident person. Only if, for some extraordinary reasons, the child can not be cared for by the parents would any other arrangement be considered. Even when the child is old enough for enrollment in a program of formal education, there are many advantages to keeping the child at home and having him attend special classes in his own community.

If, when he is old enough for school, no local facilities for deaf children are available, you will want to investigate the programs of both public (state supported) and private schools. Many schools have excellent programs that afford a deaf child the special educational help that he needs.

27. When should the education of the deaf child begin?

The sooner the better! There is much that the parents can do to help make the deaf child aware of sound and language, long before he enters school. Formal education should begin at the earliest possible age. Some formal education may begin when a child is three years old, provided that he is toilet-trained and can feed himself. At any rate, the longer we wait, the more the child will be handicapped. For example, the child with normal hearing has a vocabulary of about 2,000 words by the time he enters school, but a deaf child often enters school with no vocabulary unless his parents have been aware of his needs and have helped him learn to read lips. Even then, he will not be able to say more than a fraction of the words he can understand through lip-reading.

There are advantages to enrolling a deaf child in a nursery school program. If a nursery school program for deaf children is not available, he may be enrolled in a nursery school for hearing children provided the teacher understands the problem and is sympathetic. The nursery school program will provide a great deal of help in developing language concepts, in learning to follow directions, adjust to routines, and to play with other children. Usually children who have had this experience attack new tasks with more enthusiasm and greater confidence than do the children who have not attended a nursery school.

28. Are special classes for the deaf child available?

Your school authorities can tell you whether or not there is a special class in your area. Because the number of deaf children is small, rural areas and smaller communities do not have enough deaf children to form a class and employ a teacher who is professionally prepared. In such cases, consideration should be given to enrolling the child in a residential school for deaf children.

Special educational provisions are essential if the child is to develop his abilities. Beyond all the important things that parents can do, highly specialized methods and techniques are required for helping a deaf child develop speech and language concepts. Speech-reading lessons are necessary. Since he cannot hear, he will need to depend on reading much more than the hearing child does, and a special teacher is needed to teach him how to read. And of course he will need a great deal of help if he is to learn to speak a language he can not hear.

A deaf child may be left in the regular classroom, but that is what happens—he gets left. His native abilities are not developed. On the other hand, in a special room or special school for deaf children, he has companionship with people who understand his problem, and he gets the help that he needs for acquiring the education and the skills that will help to make him a well-adjusted, self-sufficient member of the community.

A few deaf children develop such skill in speech and lip-reading that they are able to return to the regular classroom. Others will need to continue their education with teachers who are adequately prepared to help them. All deaf children deserve the opportunities that special education offers.

29. What is meant by "the speech range"?

The normal, healthy ear of a young adult can hear tones over a range that extends from about 20 vibrations per second to about

Figure 11: More and more public schools are including as a part of their special education programs classes for children who have severe auditory handicaps.

20,000 vibrations per second. (Some animals can hear sounds as high as 50,000 vibrations per second.) As we grow older we lose some of our hearing acuity; many adults cannot hear tones of more than 10,000 or 12,000 vibrations per second.

The "speech range" refers to that portion of the total hearing range that is important for speech. Most of the energy of speech is in the range of 250 to 4000 vibrations per second; in fact, much of a conversation can be understood if one can hear only the tones of 500 to 2000 vibrations per second. Of course, with parts of the complex sounds of speech eliminated it will not sound the same, but most of it can be understood. This may be illustrated by the difference between the old fashioned pre-electric phonographs and modern "hi-fi" units. The old fashioned type could be understood (often with some difficulty) even though it reproduced only the narrow range of sounds from 300 to 3000 vibrations per second; whereas our modern record players reproduce sounds in the range of 60 to 5000. You know how different many voices sound over a telephone? Telephones reproduce sounds from 250 to 2750 vibrations per second.

A mild loss in the speech range may not be much of a handicap to an adult who has good speech, but the same amount of loss in a young child may seriously interfere with his learning of speech.

30. What does a "loss of 65 db" mean?

The intensity of a tone, the amount of energy that is present, is measured in decibels, which is usually abbreviated to "db." The reading of "0 db" on the hearing loss dial of an audiometer indicates that the equipment is sending out a signal just barely loud enough for the average, healthy, normal ear to hear in a very quiet room.

If the hearing loss dial must be turned to 15 db before a person can hear the signal, that person does not hear quite as well as the *average* person with normal hearing. Many persons have mild hearing losses of 10 or 15 db. Although this is not a significant loss, you can see that it may make some difference for a whisper is only 10 or 15 db in power or "loudness."

Conversational speech, as heard at a distance of 10 or 15 feet, is about 60 decibels. Not all speech is equally loud. We emphasize some words by saying them louder, and we stress or accent syllables. Furthermore, vowels are stronger or "carry more power" than most of the consonants, and are, therefore, easier to hear.

A person with a 65 db loss in the speech range would not be able to hear ordinary conversation. He might hear some of the louder fragments, but he would not hear enough of what was said to understand it. A person with a 50 db loss would hear conversational speech about as distinctly as a normal ear would hear a whisper.

Even a loss of 30 decibels would make speech seem indistinct—as though it were coming from a considerable distance, and the weaker parts would not be heard at all. There would, of course, be considerable strain and some misunderstanding. Such a loss would be a mild handicap for an adult, but would be a much greater handicap to a child who is trying to learn speech.

Incidentally, "a 65 db loss in the speech range" indicates that the average loss for that person in the speech frequencies is 65 decibels; his hearing may be better in some portions and poorer in other portions of the range tested.

31. How much of a loss must there be to justify a hearing aid?

That depends upon the type of loss and a number of other factors. An audiologist can best advise you concerning your child. In general it may be said that a child who is learning speech will profit from a hearing aid if he has a loss of 25 db or more in the speech range. Adults with a hearing loss of 30 db may "get by" without an aid, particularly if they have some skill at lip-reading. Anyone with a loss of between 35 and 75 db should definitely use a hearing aid. With a loss of 75 to 95 db, a hearing aid may be of considerable help, but it is doubtful if any aid will enable the person with such a loss to understand speech satisfactorily (they will need lip-reading to supplement what they hear) . With a loss greater than 95 db, a hearing aid can be expected to do little more than keep the person aware of the world of sound around him. (Even these sounds will be heard imperfectly, but it is important to keep him in as close touch as possible with his environment.)

The use of a hearing aid will not solve all hearing problems. For some people, before speech becomes loud enough to be heard it is too loud for comfort or even painful. Another difficulty is the phenomenon called "recruitment." This means that the person experiences a sudden increase in loudness that is out of proportion to the increase in the intensity of the tone. Perhaps you have tried talking to an elderly person who said, "Speak up! I don't hear so good." You talked a little louder, and he said, "Don't shout! I ain't deaf." He may have been experiencing recruitment. At your normal level of talking, he couldn't hear you clearly. But when you talked a little louder, it suddenly became too loud for him. You can see that it would be difficult for a person with this type of hearing loss to get maximum benefit from a hearing aid. When he increases the volume enough so that he can hear you, the sound suddenly becomes unbearably loud. We don't understand exactly why this phenomenon occurs in some cases, but we know that it does! A third problem involves the ability to discriminate between sounds. Some persons find it difficult to understand speech even when they report that it is "plenty loud." For these and other reasons it is sometimes necessary to have a trial period to determine just how much benefit will be derived from a hearing aid.

32. *What is the most important thing for parents to do for a deaf child?*

Accept him just as he is—hearing loss included—and love him for what he is: your child. You're disappointed that he isn't "perfect"? Of course! You're concerned about his education and his future happiness? Naturally! But he *is* your child. He can bring you much happiness and—with your understanding guidance—will give you many reasons to be proud of him. Let him know that he has a warm and secure place in your affections and in your home, and he will be well on the road to finding a comfortable place in the community.

There is no need for feelings of embarrassment or shame in acknowledging his handicap. There is no energy to waste in feelings of pity or self-pity. He is a child, with all of a child's problems and needs. His difficulty with communication will make the solution of some of the problems more complex, but they can be solved—and the role of the parents is of prime importance. Making him feel secure in your love because you accept him and are proud of him is the first step.

Of course you will want to consult a special education center or some person qualified to give you advice concerning the education of young deaf children. It may be suggested that you join a group of parents of deaf children so that you may share your experiences with them and learn together. We'll have some suggestions of things for you to do, but the most important thing is to love and accept your child just as he is.

33. *What about my feelings of rejection—do others feel that way?*

Don't you think that most parents feel the same way at times? "This is the fourth time this week that James came home with his clothes torn." "This is the fifth night in a row that Judith wouldn't go to sleep." Any time that situations seem to be unbearable, parents are apt to think, "I wish I'd never had a child!" Or, "Why did this happen to me?" An experienced social worker told me that in counselling with parents, particularly the parents of children with some handicap, this question of rejection is sure to arise.

As one mother said, "There are times when I hate her. Then I hate myself for hating her. No decent mother should feel the way I feel." But they do! Whatever differences exist are in frequency and degree!

Perhaps the most helpful thing to do in the circumstances is to face and acknowledge these negative feelings. If you recognize them, and don't try to fool yourself into thinking that they don't exist, there is not much danger of their doing harm. Psychologists tell us that the real danger lies in denying that these feelings exist; when we do that, they fester inside us until they erupt in some way. But if we acknowledge their presence, and recognize that just about everybody has them to some degree, we can deal with them in a way that does not injure the child or our relationship with the child.

Don't be a pessimistic perfectionist! We aren't perfect. We don't know all the answers. We can't see inside the child to know just how he is interpreting or reacting. We will make some mistakes. But we love him; we want what is best for him, and we will do our best.

It isn't easy to suddenly face the fact that your child is deaf;

to be forced to change your picture of the future. But it can still be a beautiful, satisfying picture. The child's future—and yours—will depend to a large extent on what you do during his early years. Seldom is there any reason for parents to blame themselves for the child's handicap. Certainly there is no possible reason to blame the child. He will need all of the love and help that you can give him—and in the giving you can find great satisfaction.

There will be times when you ask, "Why did this happen to my child?" or, "Why did God do this to me?" Don't be ashamed of such feelings. Don't feel guilty about them. It will probably help if you talk to your minister, priest, or rabbi, or talk to your doctor. If a social worker is available at a family service agency or child guidance clinic, talk to him or her. Social workers are accustomed to meeting reactions of resentment of the present and fear of the future.

But no matter how you feel, don't make the child suffer for something he can't help. His handicap of not being able to hear should not be complicated by your rejection. He must have the security that only your love and acceptance can provide.

Don't concentrate so much on the problem of deafness that you overlook all of the ways in which he is a normal child, with a child's needs. Hearing is important. But it isn't everything. Not by a long shot!

34. Should a deaf child play with hearing children?

Of course! Being familiar with the normal growth or development patterns of children will help you to understand their interests and characteristics, and this will help you in arranging for your child to have the fun and the stimulation that other children can provide.

There is really no problem for very young children. They play "side-by-side" rather than "together." That is, they tend to play independently—they may be in the same sandpile, but each makes his own castle and in the building may chatter about what he is doing. You may want to arrange "cutting and pasting" activities, or other "games" that are not dependent upon verbal communication.

A little later there will be some problems. For one thing, your deaf child will not be able to play games that depend upon auditory cues. Take hide-and-seek for an example: he would not hear the call, "All out are in free," and so may remain in hiding. He may not understand the arguments that inevitably take place—"I caught you." "No you didn't." "I did, too. You were back of the tree."

There are several things you can do to help. First, explain frankly and directly to the other children just what he can or cannot hear. Nothing is gained and many problems are created by trying to "cover-up" or deny the existence of a hearing loss. If he wears a hearing aid, demonstrate it to the others; let them examine it and listen through it while you explain that it is like a little radio. Explain, too, that since he does not hear he will not always understand how the game is played or what they want him to do. Experience has demonstrated that most children are surprisingly understanding and sympathetic. Oh, there will be a few who react unfavorably to anything or anyone who "is different." We can understand this if we examine our own reactions to the child who drools because he has cerebral palsy and cannot control the muscles used in swallowing, or to the boy who stutters, or has a physical deformity. Fortunately, younger children are often more accepting of differences than adults are. Our own matter-of-fact explanation will help in this direction.

A second thing that you can do to help is to explain to the parents of other children in the neighborhood. If you explain the problem to them, explain Jimmy's needs and what you are trying to do about them, you can often help other parents to a better understanding and greater acceptance, and the attitude of the parents will be reflected in the attitudes of Jimmy's playmates.

A third thing you can do is to explain the rules of the game to Jimmy. This will help him to avoid some of the mistakes that would be misunderstood and resented by other children. Sometimes, particularly if you have the friendship of other children, you will be able to suggest modifications of a game that will make it possible for Jimmy to play. For example, you may introduce a new and exciting game: playing hide-and-seek in pairs.

A fourth thing is to help him make friends. This is important enough to be dealt with under a separate heading.

35. *How can I help him make friends?*

Like most of these questions, this one deserves a much longer answer than we can give here. Let's begin by pointing out a common mistake. Because we recognize that oral communication is important, we try to explain all problems in terms of the hearing loss. We need to remember that all children have their problems, and that the deaf or hard-of-hearing child is no exception. Observe your child. Is he friendly? Does he share his toys and take his turn? Some of the misunderstanding and resentment other children show toward your child may be related to the hearing loss, but some of it may be the result of undesirable personality characteristics. These are problems that parents of all children have to face, and for which they must try to find solutions. The communication barrier may make the solution a bit more difficult where deaf children are concerned—but the problem is the same. You can help him to make friends by helping him acquire the qualities of a good friend and playmate.

Invite children to your home to play with your child. Be sure that they have interesting toys and activities. This should not be thought of as "bribing" other children to play with yours. Rather, it is just making the situation attractive; it is a matter of creating the best possible atmosphere and conditions for having a good time together. Your attitude toward the other children will be an important factor. If other children like you (and the games or swings) well enough, they will come around. In time they will get to understand your child's problem, accept it, and play with him.

One mother stated that she deliberately tried to cultivate the children who seemed more mature, more understanding—those who had a "greater capacity for friendship." You see, if only one or two playmates understand the problem, and like your child well enough to go to the extra bother of communicating with him, he is well on the way to belonging to the group.

36. *How can I answer his question, "Why don't they like me?"*

Sometimes parents wonder how to answer such questions as "Why don't they like me?" and "Why don't they want to play with me?" Our tendency, I believe, is to exclaim, "Oh! If he could only hear!" But as has been pointed out before, the hearing loss is not always the problem. It may be wise to try to find out if the communication barrier is responsible for this bit of unhappiness. Sometimes it will be. Sometimes no one in the group thinks to explain to the deaf child. Sometimes no one wants to take the time and the trouble to explain. If it does seem to be a problem of hearing you might say, "Maybe you did not hear something that Bobby said. Bobby didn't know that you didn't hear him. Remember last week? Bobby asked you not to ride his tricycle. You didn't hear him, so you rode it. That made him angry with you." Or, "Maybe they told you where they were going and you didn't hear them. Remember yesterday the children all ran off and left you when they heard the fire engine. No one thought to tell you. Most people want to be friendly, but sometimes they forget that you don't hear them."

"Most people want to be friendly"—but we must be realistic. Children can be cruel. There are times when they seem to delight in running off and leaving or hiding from some playmate. Most children—hearing as well as deaf—come home at times with the complaint, "They won't let me play." Sometimes it helps if we ask the child, "What do you think the trouble was?" His answer may suggest one of several answers: That boy next door certainly is a bully! Or, I must help my boy learn to share and take his turn. Or, I must have the children in for some games and try again to help them understand that my boy doesn't hear.

All of us will be happier if we learn how to tolerate, to live with frustration, for all of us will encounter it. Because of his difficulty with communication, the deaf child may meet more of it, but we cannot always shield him. He must learn "in life's hard school" that he will meet with many disappointments. One of the most valuable contributions we can make toward his becoming a happy adult is in helping him develop a tolerance for frustration.

Tolerance for frustration just means that we learn to "take things in our stride." Of course you will want to be sure that your child is not being selfish or disagreeable. But the fact remains that some difficulties are inescapable, no matter how near perfect you are. We want to be sympathetic, but not overly-protective. We must face the situation realistically and directly, and by our own matter-of-fact manner help the child to develop greater tolerance for the frustrations that are sure to come. We cannot start in this direction too soon.

37. *What hearing aid should I buy?*

There are many good hearing aids on the market. To help you decide what hearing aid is best for your child it would be well to visit a hearing clinic or hearing center. Sometimes a hearing aid salesman advertises under the name of "Greenville Hearing Clinic" or "Green County Hearing Center." These names are misleading. The kind of center or clinic recommended here is one that is operated by a college or by some community agency. *It does not sell any hearing aid.* It sells (or gives) only the service of helping you decide what make and model aid will best meet your child's needs.

Frequently it is recommended that for very young children a desk-type hearing aid (or desk amplifier) be used. Such an aid is larger than a wearable aid and is typically capable of producing higher fidelity at greater intensities than the smaller aids. These amplifiers use earphones that fit over the ears (like a pilot wears) rather than in the ear (like the conventional hearing aid).

If the advice of a clinic or hearing center is not available, but you have been advised by the special teacher or audiologist to have your child use amplification, here are some points to consider:

(1) *Cost.* Of course we usually "get what we pay for." But in the selection of a hearing aid, the most expensive is not necessarily the one that best meets the needs of a particular patient. Sometimes the difference in cost reflects a fancier case rather than better amplification. Sometimes the greater cost reflects features that are not needed.

(2) *Reputation.* Generally, you are safer in purchasing the product of a manufacturer who has been in the business for a number of years, rather than a newcomer to the field. The same is true of the local dealer or salesman. Admittedly, the fact that he has been in business for twenty years is no guarantee that he will not go out of business tomorrow. However, there are advantages to having a local representative available, and the fact that he is well established

is about as good assurance as you can get that he will continue. Besides, if he has been in business for some years, you can talk to some of his customers. Are they satisfied with the hearing aid? with the service? with the treatment they receive?

(3) *Availability of service.* Modern hearing aids are a tremendous improvement over the hearing aids of fifteen years ago, and manufacturers are constantly trying to improve their products. But things do go wrong. Batteries burn out. Cords break. Accidents happen. How soon can you get it repaired? Some hearing aid dealers have their own repair or service departments. Others must send the damaged aid to the factory. Some will lend you an aid to use while yours is being repaired. This is a matter you will want to investigate before you decide what aid to purchase.

Other questions and answers related to the ear and its functions are found in the next chapter.

chapter vii

the ear and its functions

1. How do we hear?

MANY PARENTS ASK, "What causes a hearing loss?" That question can best be answered after we briefly describe the ear and its functions.

If you dropped a pebble into a quiet pool, ripples would spread out in all directions. The ripples (or little waves) would rock a floating leaf without moving it toward shore, for the surface of the water is not moving. A moment later the ripples would reach the reeds growing in the water's edge and cause them to wave gently to and fro. Someone farther away from the pool might see the reeds waving and think, "Something disturbed the water."

This is a simplified analogy of the hearing process. As the pebble set up ripples in the pool, a vibrating object sets up sound waves in the air. It may be a violin string, a siren, or the vocal folds in the larynx (or voice box) . These vibrations or sound waves travel through the air at a speed of about 1100 feet per second. (The speed varies somewhat with atmospheric conditions.) It is the wave that travels—not the air itself.

Have you watched children standing in line? The boy at the end pushes forward, and the movement is transmitted from one child to the next until the child first in line is pushed against the door. No child moves to amount to anything, but the wave of pressure moves along the line. In much the same way the vibrating object pushes the molecules of air that are next to it, and they in turn push the molecules next to them—and the wave spreads out.

The ear is divided into three parts, called the outer ear, the middle ear, and the inner ear. The outer ear is composed of the external ear or auricle (the part that we see) and the auditory or external canal. The external ear serves as a funnel to collect the sound waves and direct them into the auditory canal. The inner end of the canal is closed by the thin tympanic membrane—the ear drum. When the sound waves strike against the ear drum they cause it to vibrate (much as the waves on the pond caused the reeds to move).

The middle ear is a small cavity which is lined with mucous membrane. It contains three tiny bones that are called *ossicles*. The first of these, the hammer, is attached to the ear drum. When the ear drum vibrates, the hammer moves and causes the second bone in the chain (the anvil) to vibrate. The anvil, in turn, moves the third bone, the stirrup. The footplate of the stirrup is attached to the membrane that covers an opening to the inner ear. This opening through the bony wall of the inner ear is called the oval window. Thus, when the sound waves coming through the ear strike the ear drum and cause it to vibrate, the ossicles, acting as levers, transmit the vibrations across the middle ear to the oval window of the inner ear. We should also mention that the middle ear is connected to the throat by the Eustachian tube. This tube is closed

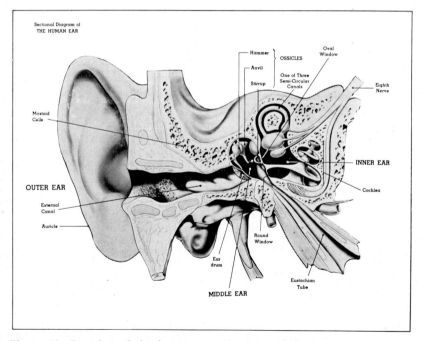

Figure 12: Drawing of the human ear. Courtesy of Sonotone Corporation, Elmsford, New York.

or collapsed most of the time, but it opens during the act of swallowing or yawning to equalize the air pressure in the middle ear with the external air pressure. (That's why the airline stewardess gives you gum to chew.) Then, too, oxygen is absorbed from the air in the middle ear, and is replenished through the Eustachian tube.

The inner ear is even more complex. In its bony capsule it contains not only an intricate portion of the hearing mechanism (the cochlea), but also the sensory organ for balance (including the three semi-circular canals). Since these are so closely connected and even send their signals or nerve impulses along the same cranial nerve, it is not surprising that a poor sense of equilibrium is sometimes associated with a hearing loss.

The cochlea, the part of the inner ear that is concerned with hearing, is rather like a snail shell in appearance. The entire inner ear is filled with fluid. We need not concern ourselves with the intricasies of the inner ear, except to note that it is divided into sections by membranes running lengthwise (around its two and three-quarter turns). On one of these membranes there are thousands of tiny hair cells. These are connected with nerve fibers which unite to form the auditory nerve which is called the acoustic branch of the VIIIth cranial nerve.

Above the membrane with the hair cells is the oval window, and below it is the round window. Both would open into the middle ear if they were not closed by membranes.

Now, let's start a sound wave and observe what happens. The sound wave travels through the air toward us. The external ear funnels it into the auditory canal where it encounters the ear drum and makes it vibrate. The ossicles carry the vibrations across the middle ear and push in on the oval window. This increases the pressure on the liquid in the inner ear. Te relieve this pressure the round window bulges out into the middle ear. When the oval window returns to its resting position, the pressure on the fluid of the inner ear is released and the round window loses its bulge. This is repeated for the next sound wave. When we realize that the normal ear can hear tones that consist of about 20 vibrations per second to tones of about 20,000 vibrations per second, it seems little short of fantastic!

What happens in the inner ear is still not completely understood. It is known that the tiny hair cells "feel" or move with the vibrations of the fluid that surrounds them, but questions concerning how sound is analyzed in terms of pitch, intensity (or loudness), and complexity (as when we hear an entire orchestra) cannot be answered at present. (There are several fascinating theories, but none is universally accepted.)

For our purposes, it is enough to know that in the inner ear the mechanical movement or vibrations are converted to nerve impulses that are transmitted to the brain where they are interpreted as sound. When this happens, we say, "I hear!"

With so complex a mechanism that must operate at such terrific speed, it is not surprising that various things can go wrong and cause different types of hearing impairment or loss.

2. What is conductive loss?

Conductive (or conduction) loss of hearing results from the sound waves or vibrations not being transmitted to the nerve fibers of the inner ear. In other words, something interferes with the conduction of the vibrations so that they do not reach the inner ear.

3. What is perceptive loss?

Perceptive (or nerve) loss of hearing is present when the vibrations of sound are properly transmitted through the ear canal, across the middle ear to the oval window of the inner ear, but something "goes wrong" either in the inner ear or along the pathway of the nerve to the brain. That is to say, the outer and middle ear are functioning normally, but there is some impairment of the inner ear or the nerve that interferes with hearing.

4. What is a mixed loss?

When part of the hearing loss is of the conductive type and part of the perceptive type, it is referred to as "mixed." In such a case, not all of the available sound reaches the inner ear, and not all of the sound that reaches the inner ear is received by the brain.

5. *What is a flat loss?*

You recall that the normal ear can hear sound over a wide range of pitch or frequency. Usually in testing hearing only the frequencies between 125 and 12,000 vibrations per second are tested. If there is a loss, but all of these frequencies are heard equally well (or nearly so) the loss is said to be "flat."

6. *What is a regional loss?*

If the hearing loss for some frequencies is much greater than the loss at other frequencies, the loss is referred to as "regional." Usually it is the high frequencies that are affected in a loss of this type; in fact, the term, "high frequency loss" means a "regional loss" in the high frequencies.

As is stated elsewhere, a regional hearing loss may go undetected in a child. He hears enough of speech to respond to it, so you know that "he hears me when I talk to him." But he may not hear the consonant sounds, or not hear them distinctly, and his own speech reflects the confusion of sounds. You see, vowels are made up primarily of the low frequencies, and consonants are made up primarily of high frequencies.

The child with a flat hearing loss hears clearly and distinctly when you speak loudly enough. The child with a regional loss will hear speech of normal intensity or loudness, but he will hear it imperfectly. He will, of course, learn to speak no more distinctly than your speech sounds to him—unless he receives special help.

7. *What causes a hearing loss?*

(1) *Causes of Conductive Loss.* Most of the acquired hearing losses in children are of the conductive type; that is, they result from some dysfunction of the outer or middle ear.

(a) *Conditions of the outer ear.* Sometimes a child is born with no auricle (the external part of the ear), with the auditory canal closed by a layer of skin, or with no auditory canal at all. This condition is called *congenital atresia,* and is sometimes accompanied by a malformation of the middle ear. Modern surgery can do fantastic things! It can fashion an external ear to provide normal appearance. It can even create an auditory canal. How effective these measures will be in restoring hearing depends largely upon the condition of the middle ear and the inner ear. An otologist (or ear specialist) should be consulted.

A much more common difficulty with the outer ear is the blocking of the canal by excess wax or by some foreign object (such as a bean, a wad of paper or cotton). The ear wax (or cerumen) is produced by tiny glands, probably for the purpose of catching dust and tiny insects before they get deeper into the ear. But some ears produce so much wax that it clogs or blocks the canal. This results in some loss of hearing.

It is a simple matter for a physician to remove excess wax from the ears, and usually a foreign object can be removed without much difficulty. However, it is extremely dangerous for you to prod or dig with a hairpin, pencil, tweezers, or other "instruments." There is too much danger of scratching the delicate skin that lines the canal, and that means danger of infection. There is also the danger that you may damage the ear drum. You've probably heard your grandmother say, "Don't put anything in your ear smaller than your elbow." That's good advice!

(b) *Conditions of the middle ear.* Probably the most common cause of hearing loss of the conductive type is *otitis media;* this is an inflammation or infection of the middle ear. When a child complains of an earache there's a strong possibility that he has *otitis media.* The Eustachian tubes connect the middle ear and the nasopharynx or back of the throat, so it is a direct path for infections of the upper respiratory tract (colds, sore-throat, and the like) to the middle ear. Recurring infections or the development of a chronic infection may cause permanent damage to the hearing mechanism. Still another danger is that the infection may spread from the middle ear to the mastoid process, and from there to the covering of the brain (causing meningitis).

Otosclerosis is a disease that affects the bony portion of the inner ear. Eventually, damage may be done to the hearing mechanism of the inner ear, but in its earlier stages it is more frequently characterized by the growth of a spongy bone that spreads into the middle ear. When this occurs, the tiny bones or ossicles (particularly the stirrup) cannot move freely to transmit vibrations to the oval window of the inner ear.

Medical and surgical treatment can usually improve the hearing of persons with conductive loss, and sometimes the complete restoration of hearing is possible. Only an ear specialist (an otologist or otolaryngologist) can determine just what treatment is needed. Even if hearing cannot be restored, it is important to stop the infection before further damage occurs. For this reason an ear specialist should be consulted as soon as possible after the presence of an infection or a hearing loss is detected. In fact, the proper functioning of our ears is so important that I would consult the specialist as soon as a hearing loss or infection was *suspected*.

(2) *Causes of Perceptive Loss.* Perceptive loss results from dysfunction of the inner ear or the auditory nerve.

(a) *Congenital causes.* Strictly speaking, a distinction may be made between "hereditary" and "congenital;" hereditary meaning "transmitted by the germ plasma or genes," and congenital meaning "acquired during development in the uterus." We use the term "congenital causes" to include all factors operating before the birth of the child. Heredity probably accounts for some cases of perceptive hearing loss. Some studies reveal that when both parents have congenital deafness (which is not explained in terms of the mother's illness during pregnancy), they are more likely to have children with congenital deafness than are parents who were not congenitally deaf.

If a mother suffers certain diseases during her pregnancy (particularly during the first three months) the embryo is subject to various sorts of injury. German measles (rubella) is known to produce deafness, blindness, cleft palate, cerebral palsy, and mental deficiency in the embryo. Other diseases, such as influenza, may also have harmful effects on the unborn child.

(b) *Acquired causes.* Diseases such as mumps, measles, diphtheria, scarlet fever, whooping cough, influenza, and "virus infections" may all cause a loss of hearing. If an inflammation in the nasal passage or throat spreads through the Eustachian tube to the middle ear the loss is of the conductive type, but if the nerve endings of the inner ear are affected the loss is of the perceptive type. Meningitis and encephalitis may also damage the inner ear.

Occasionally an accident (automobile wreck or explosion) may fracture the temporal bone and damage the inner ear, resulting in a perceptive type hearing loss. Many cases of perceptive loss are due to another kind of trauma: loud noise. Intense noise, experienced for even a brief period, may result in damage to the nerve fibers of the inner ear. Industry is devoting much time and money to the control of noise in factories in an effort to avoid "industrial deafness" resulting from exposure to noise. It may be wise for those who operate farm tractors or other noisy equipment to wear earplugs that would somewhat reduce the danger of damaging the hearing processes of the inner ear.

A third cause of acquired perceptive loss is the toxic effect of drugs. When quinine was used extensively for the treatment of a cold or malaria, it was responsible for considerable hearing loss. Today it is probably streptomycin (and its derivatives) that is the biggest offender among the drugs. Physicians are aware of the danger to hearing and prescribe this drug only as a life-saving measure.

Unfortunately, not much can be done for perceptive hearing loss. It is, however, advisable to see an ear specialist as soon as the symptoms of hearing loss are detected, even though the medical care may be directed toward the prevention of further loss, rather than the restoration of normal hearing.

chapter viii

suggestions for helping
a child who is hard of hearing

suggestions to the teacher

Eᴠᴇʀʏ ᴛᴇᴀᴄʜᴇʀ ɪɴ ᴛʜᴇ regular classroom will have some contact with a child who has a hearing loss. In the past, these children were often thought of as stupid, lazy, or troublemakers; and the hearing loss—the cause of the difficulty—went unnoticed. With the extension of special services, the improvement of diagnostic techniques, and the increased awareness and sensitivity of today's teachers, more and more hearing handicapped children are receiving the understanding and sympathetic consideration that make their educational experiences both happier and more meaningful.

As you read the suggestions offered below, you will discover that they do not make excessive demands on your time. Rather, they will help you to understand the problem and enable you to teach the child more effectively.

Seat the hard-of-hearing child toward the front of the room. If hearing is better in one ear than in the other, the better one should be toward the source of sound (teacher and class).

Permit the child to move his seat if the "teaching center" moves to another part of the room. Permit him to turn around to hear other pupils speak.

Help him with his lip-reading. Most of us find it easier to understand a speaker when we can see him. That's partly because, whether we know it or not, we are doing some lip-reading. The hard-of-hearing child has even more need to see the speaker's face. We can help him by seating him where he will be from six to ten feet away from the place where we do most of our talking. If he is seated and we stand too close, he looks up to see our chin and nose and gets only a distorted view of the lips. We will also want to keep our hands away from our faces when speaking, and if we read from a book, we will want to keep the book from interfering with the child's view of

114

our lips. We will allow the light to shine on our faces, not in the pupil's eyes. (This means that we will keep away from the window!)

Do not turn your back while talking. Do not talk while writing on the chalkboard. Do not walk about the room while talking about important phases of school work. Select the spot that is most ad-vantageous for the hard-of-hearing child.

Avoid using loud tones or exaggerated mouth movements. Speak naturally and use very few gestures. Gestures draw attention away from the face and lips which the child must watch.

Many words sound the same (blue, blew; tax, tacks). This is confusing enough. But many words that do not *sound* the same *look* the same on the lips. For example: bat, pat, and mat *look* alike, as do bad, pad, mad. Nimble, nipple, nibble *look* alike on the lips. Words that *look* alike are called "homophenes." There are hundreds of them to add to the confusion of a child who is reading lips. Knowing this, we will understand why even an expert at speech-reading misunderstands directions or questions. It is essential, therefore, that when dictating spelling words, we use them in sentences to give the pupil a clue.

Just one sentence will increase our sympathy for the problems of the person who is trying to read lips. In the sentence given below, each word in a column looks *on the lips* exactly like every word in the column. Try to figure out what was "said."

Baby	meet	hid	the	pair	because	he*	was	ban.
Maybe	beat	hint		bare			it	man.
	bead	hit		bear (noun)				mad.
	bean			bear (verb)				pad.
	Pete			pare				mat.
	mean			mare				pat.
	meat			pear				pan.
	beet							bat.
								bad.

---

*Actually, *he* and *it* are not homophenes—they do not look alike *on the lips* when they are carefully articulated, but in rapid speech (the way most of us talk), there's not enough difference to readily distinguish between them.

With the above sentence in print so that we can take our time to sort through the words and try various combinations, we discover that there are numerous possibilities. It is fairly easy to eliminate some of the words completely. Some other combinations are rather unlikely, but you can't be sure.

The lip-reader doesn't have this time to sort through and experiment. No wonder he becomes confused and discouraged. No wonder he misunderstands.

 It is usually helpful to explain to other children that many words look alike, and that Jimmy or Susan will sometimes make mistakes for that reason. Write some homophenes on the chalkboard (bill, pill, mill, or bit, bid, mit, pit), then say one word without voice—that is, just "mouth" the word but without sound. Let the class try to tell which word you said. Most of them will be wrong, for there is no possible way to tell except by guessing. This procedure will help others in the class to understand the problem of the hard-of-hearing child, and understanding helps eliminate teasing and unfair judgments.

Do not proceed too far in a discussion without asking or making sure that the hard-of-hearing child understands. If he does not understand, restate the material in a different way. Perhaps he was not familiar with the key words that you used, or some of them may have "looked like" other words.

Names of people and places are very difficult for the hard-of-hearing to understand. It is well to place new words or terms on the board and discuss new material from this vocabulary. (Children with good hearing often benefit from this approach.)

 Ask another child to help the hard-of-hearing child get the correct assignment. The teacher should not, however, expect the helping child to devote a great deal of time to this. Also, care should be taken to see that the hard-of-hearing child does not become too dependent on the helper.

Use clear enunciation and insist that the pupils do so. Look at yourself in the mirror while you talk. If your lips and jaw have little or no movement, the hard-of-hearing child will not be able to read your lips. On the other hand, exaggerated movements should be avoided. They're confusing.

Encourage participation in extra-curricular activities, especially vocal music. The hard-of-hearing child tends to withdraw from others. We can help him widen his circle of friends and achieve better adjustment by making participation in various activities seem attractive.

The hard-of-hearing child needs sympathetic understanding. He tires more easily than other children because of the eye strain and the strain of listening to what is only partially heard. We can help by planning the day's work so that the periods when he must "pay attention" are interspersed with other activities.

Encourage the hard-of-hearing child to keep trying. Be patient. Repeat instructions as often as necessary. He needs confidence, and this can be built by helping him discover his abilities and talents and by guiding him into activities where he can achieve his share of success.

If a visit is being planned, or a visitor is coming, anticipate the difficulty that the hard-of-hearing child will have and prepare him for it. Help him become familiar with the names of persons or objects he will be seeing. Explain any special rules ahead of time when you can be sure that he understands them. (Incidentally, this procedure will make a trip more meaningful for the whole class—and a lot easier on you!)

Nurses and teachers should be especially vigilant in noting common colds, influenza, or throat infections in the hard-of-hearing child. He should be given medical attention as quickly as possible. Everything must be done to prevent further hearing loss, which may result from infections spreading to the middle ear through the Eustachian tubes.

Hard-of-hearing children require special help in language activities such as reading and spelling because they do not hear all of the sounds. They will probably need extra help in building adequate vocabularies.

suggestions to the parents

With slight modifications, the suggestions given to the classroom teacher in the preceding section will be helpful to you. Some of the suggestions already made can be carried out only if you give your cooperation. You will want to read all of them, and it would be a good idea to discuss them with the classroom teacher.

There are, however, some things that the parents can do better than anyone else.

Help the child develop a sense of humor. Don't laugh at his mistakes, but try to get him to laugh at them. Help him to see that some of the situations that arise are funny. One way to do this is to tell him little jokes on yourself. The joke may or may not involve speech. For example, my wife laughs as heartily as I do whenever we think of the time she kissed me goodbye at the door at seven o'clock in the morning and said, "Well, goodnight, dear." Recently I called to her and said, "Please bring me some thread." She answered, "Do you mind waiting just a minute? I'll fix you a sandwich." I don't remember how old I was before I learned that the name of the famous geyser in Yellowstone National Park is Old Faithful—not Old Facefull.

Preview some of his lessons with him. This will be most effective if you are cooperating with the classroom teacher. By keeping just a little ahead of his classwork in reading, history, social studies, etc., and by talking about the interesting or important portions, you help him to become familiar with the central ideas and with the proper names (that are almost always difficult for lip-readers).

Help him to be a happy, well-adjusted child. You'll find some suggestions on page 61-64 (What Can I Do To Help When There Is No Speech Correctionist?). Most of these suggestions will be applicable to the hard-of-hearing child.

Try to anticipate situations that may be difficult for him and prepare him for them. If you are going to have a guest, be sure that he knows the name and relationship. Be sure he knows how to greet the guest. Children with good hearing learn a lot by just hearing what other people say. The hard-of-hearing child misses a lot of this casual sort of learning. You can make things easier for him if you prepare him for changes in the routine and make sure that he knows what to expect.

You will be able to find more time than the classroom teacher for helping your child learn to read lips. Some helpful hints are offered in the suggestions to teachers beginning on page 114. In addition, your speech correctionist, public health nurse, local library, or a source to which the school authorities can refer you will be able to provide further help along this line.

Help him with his lip-reading. If he is receiving help at school, you can cooperate with his teacher. If he is a pre-school child, the suggestions offered in the section for helping deaf children to learn lip-reading can be used. Even if his hearing is made functional by the use of a hearing aid, the ability to read lips will be of great value to any child with a hearing loss.

Sometimes when we talk louder in our efforts to make a hard-of-hearing child hear us, our voices sound angry. I know of one child who developed a great dislike for her mother because the only thing she ever heard her mother say was, "No! No!" The mother often said things that all parents say, "I love you. You're a sweet child. Your hair is so pretty." But these words were spoken softly, and the child never heard them! If you have to talk loud when you say, "No" or "Don't," be sure you talk equally loud when you say, "I love you." It isn't easy. But it's mighty important for the child to know that he is loved.

suggestions for helping a child who is deaf

Perhaps the very beginning of help for the deaf child is the realization that he is a child. He is like other children in many ways. His emotional, social, and educational needs are basically the same as the needs of all children. The primary difference is his lack of hearing. Sometimes we become so concerned about the difference that we lose sight of all the similarities. Sometimes we are so aware of the hearing loss that we fail to meet all of the other needs. And, interestingly enough, these basic needs of both hearing and deaf children can best be met in much the same ways. Let us resolve, then, to think not of the *"deaf child,"* but of the *"child— who is deaf."* In other words, let's think of him first of all as a child and treat him as a child. We will neither ignore nor deny the deafness, but that is of secondary importance. His needs as a child come first.

A second point to remember is that children—all children—learn most efficiently and most happily through first hand experience. We can talk about a dog, and we can show pictures of dogs, but a child really learns what a dog is by playing with a dog, petting his soft fur, feeling his cold nose, being "kissed" by his warm tongue, and perhaps feeling his sharp teeth when the tail is pulled. A child is interested in the texture and warmth of mashed potatoes and in the way they can be squeezed before he is interested in the word *potatoes.* "Potatoes" is just a label, a symbol used to refer to this interesting white heap on his plate. I feel sorry for the child who was never allowed to find out for himself what potatoes are!

Children learn best when they are experiencing, participating, exploring. We can help most not by dictating what must be learned, but by providing opportunities for learning! Children want to know about the world around them. All we need to do is to direct this natural desire to learn by providing opportunities to see, to lift, to feel, to taste. We are eager for the child to learn to read lips and to speak, but it is more important to keep alive this zest for learning!

If we can succeed in encouraging the child's zest for learning, we will have a child who is no less deaf, but is happier and more spontaneous, and certainly better adjusted to the world in which he must live than is a child who is drilled and "pressured" into learning what we want him to learn. Not that lip-reading and speech are unimportant, but he will be a happier child and a more self-sufficient adult (and probably a better speaker and reader of of lips) if we place more emphasis on his eagerness to learn, and supply the opportunities.

How much of a handicap is deafness? That question can't be answered in terms of pounds or percentages. It is rather generally agreed, however, that a great deal of the problem of deafness originates not in the loss of hearing, but in the attitudes of society. Much of the unhappiness and frustration that is experienced by persons who have any kind of impairment results from the unreasonable attitudes and expectations of others.

Audiologists can precisely measure the extent of a hearing loss. Otologists can determine the type of hearing loss. But the extent of the handicap depends to a large degree upon the over-protection, the lack of understanding, the lack of opportunity, the setting of goals that are beyond the abilities of the child, or the refusal to let the child do what he is able to do—and these, for the infant and young child, are primarily the responsibility of the parent. Lack of hearing is a handicap. But a more serious matter is the handicapped personality that results from the attitudes, evaluations, and demands of others.

This philosophy leads to the conclusions that the most important things parents can do for a child who is deaf are to love him, make him feel secure in your affection and in his home, recognize his abilities (as well as his limitations), and provide opportunities for him to learn.

With this background, what are some of the things we need to do?

help him learn to read lips

Lip-reading is often referred to as speech-reading, for much depends upon interpreting facial expressions and being aware of the situation—as well as observing the movement of the lips. How can we help a child acquire this skill?

Talk to him. Sing to him. Enjoy him. No child will learn to read lips unless there are lips to be read. It may be a good idea to re-read the suggestions for helping a child learn to talk offered in Chapter II. There we stressed the importance of the repetition of simple phrases so that the child may learn to associate certain sounds with certain activities (feeding, bathing, dressing, going to bed, and the like). These suggestions are all doubly important for the deaf child.

But the child who is deaf will need additional help. He must learn to associate meaning with the movement of the lips. Here are three "musts."

(1) Be sure that the light is on your face, not in the baby's eyes, when you talk to him. The child must be able to see the expression on your face and the movement of your lips as clearly as possible if he is to learn to associate meaning with what he sees—and this is the beginning of lip-reading.

(2) Be sure that your face is at the level of the child's. If you are so far above him that he must look up at an uncomfortable angle in order to see you, he will soon lose interest. Later on we hope that he will be able to read lips from any angle. Right now we are helping him learn to interpret speech by what he can see, and we will want to give him every advantage, so get your face down where he can see you easily and observe every visible movement.

(3) Encourage him to feel your face or throat while you talk. Most infants do this from time to time. While you hold them and talk to them they put their fingers on your face and lips. Encourage the deaf child to feel the vibrations of the cheeks and throat and the puffs of air that come from the mouth. This helps him to become aware of the changing patterns of speech, and is the first step toward encouraging him to talk.

Patience is the keynote of success. We will remember that the infant's attention span is short. We will not antagonize him by trying to force him to watch us or to keep his hand on our faces. But we will talk to him. Talk, talk, talk, and encourage others to talk to him. We will not use exaggerated mouth movements or a slow syl-la-ble by syl-la-ble tempo. Anything that is not natural speech will only confuse the child. We will talk naturally and

Figure 13: You can help the deaf child become aware of speech by encouraging him to feel the vibrations of your cheek and throat as you talk to him.

happily just as we talk to children who do not have a hearing problem.

Of course he will not understand you at first, any more than the hearing child understands what is said to him. But if you follow the suggestions of simple sentences, repeated frequently in meaningful situations, he will gradually learn to associate meaning with the movements that he sees on your face. At first he will rely primarily on the situation and get only a general meaning. This is sometimes referred to as "general lip-reading" to distinguish it from "specific lip-reading" which involves recognizing specific words. We'll get to that later. Right now we are interested in having the deaf child begin to associate certain facial expressions and movements of the lips with the things being done, just as the hearing baby forms associations between what is heard and what is done. Of course learning to distinguish the small, and often obscured, movements of the lips will take much longer than learning to distinguish words that are heard. Getting the idea from the situation is an important first step toward the specific lip-reading we want him to do later. We might think of general lip-reading as "lip-reading ideas" in contrast with "lip-reading words," and getting the idea is what's important.

Let's see how this works. Mother gets the child's attention (he can't lipread if he isn't looking at you!) and says, "We are going out, so we must put on our coats." Going to the closet and showing him, "This is my coat. This is your coat. I will help you put on your coat. Your coat will keep you warm. We will button your coat. Your coat has three buttons. Now I will put on my coat. My coat will keep me warm. Now we have on our coats. We are ready to go." In time, he will begin to associate some of the words (the lip movements that he sees) with putting on his coat and going outdoors. Eventually he will come to recognize the word "coat" when he sees it on your lips, but that comes later and is the beginning of "specific lip-reading."

Take another example. You might say, "It's bed time. It's time to go to bed. We'll take off your clothes. We'll put on your pajamas, and you'll go to bed. This is your bed. I'll put you on the bed. I'll tuck you in the bed. Good-night. Go to sleep." The next day, during playtime, you might say, "This is your dolly's bed. Put the dolly to bed. I'll help you. We'll take off the dolly's clothes, and put the dolly to bed. Now we'll put you to bed. It is time for your nap. It is time to go to bed, etc. etc." Gradually the child learns to understand the situation and knows what to expect. Slowly he learns to rely less on the situation and to get more of the meaning from the movement of your lips.

You will be tempted to make your meaning clear with panto-mime and gestures. Let's suppose you say, "Go get your ball," but he does not understand. You could point to the ball, or you could go through the motions of rolling the ball on the floor. Don't. Movements of the arms are so much bigger and easier to see than movements of the lips that he will pay more attention to the arms than to the lips. It would help him more if you take the time to say, "Let's find your ball. Where is the ball? Is this the ball? No. This is the truck. Here is your tractor. Where is the ball? Here it is! Here is the ball. This is your ball. Let's play with your ball. You sit here and I will roll the ball to you." As you proceed to play, you say, "I roll the ball. You roll the ball. I roll the ball to you. You roll the ball to me." Do not expect him to go get the ball the next time you ask him to. But with enough repetitions, day after day, the pleasant activity of playing ball becomes associated with the observed move-ment of your lips, and in time he will respond to your request, "Go get your ball."

Somewhere I heard the advice, "Learn to gesture with your eyes." That's a good idea. Let's suppose that you get your coat and the child's coat out of the closet. As you get into your coat, the child looks at your face questioningly. You say, "Put on your coat." He looks around the room, and back to you. You say, "We are going down town. Put on your coat," and direct your gaze at his coat. He follows your gaze, sees the coat, and because he has just seen you putting your coat on, he puts his coat on. You go to the door, with purse in one hand and letters in the other. You step to one side, and as he looks up at you, you say, "Open the door," and direct your gaze at the door knob. Following your gaze, he sees the door knob. What is more natural than for him to open the door? This is general lip-reading. But the time will come when he will not need to rely so much on the situation or on your "gestures with the eyes." When you say, "Put on your coat" or "Open the door" he will understand you. And that's the beginning of specific lip-reading.

A few inexpensive toys will enable you to help him learn more specific lip-reading. Is he especially fond of his red ball? Get an-other one just like it. Also get two fire engines (the minature dime-store variety), and two airplanes. At this stage of the game (and for the child it must be a game!), the objects should be of the same size and color. With two boxes or paper bags big enough to hold the objects, we are ready to begin. Show him the red ball and talk about it. "This is a ball. It is a pretty red ball. I put the ball on the table. Here is another ball. This is a ball. (Place it on the table beside the first ball, and gesture appropriately.) And this is a ball." Present the two fire engines in the same manner. Then say, "This is a ball; this is a fire engine. This is a ball; and this is a fire engine. This is my ball. I put my ball here. (Place it in your box.) This is your ball. Put your ball in your box." If he does not understand, gently guide his hand to his ball and say again, "This is your ball. Put your ball in the box," as you help him to do it. Then place one fire engine in a box as you talk about it, and direct him to do so with the other one.

There are three requirements for making this procedure into an effective learning experience: (1) It must be fun. If you can't "play this game" without becoming tense and impatient, don't play it! It must be a pleasant, rewarding experience. (2) Be sure that the names of the objects used do not "look alike" on the lips. In fact, the difference should be as great as possible. "Ball" and "bell" are too much alike. "Ball" and "shoe" would be a good combination, but "shoe" and "shell" are so similar as to make the task too difficult at this point. We want to choose objects that will make success easy. If he succeeds in doing what is expected of him, so that the experience is interesting and pleasant, he will gladly continue the game, and gradually you can introduce objects with names that "look almost alike." Try looking in the mirror. If you find it difficult to see the difference between your natural production of two words, it certainly is too difficult for the child. (3) Use objects with which the child is familiar and in which he is interested. If the object is familiar, but he doesn't like to play with it, the child is less apt to enjoy the game or even cooperate in it. If the object is fascinating but unfamiliar, he will probably be so eager to handle it and explore it that the game isn't interesting. If new objects are to be used, it is probably wise to let him play with them for a while before you start the game. It is also desirable to keep the objects used in this game set apart, to be used only for this and similar activities.

When he can distinguish readily between "ball" and "fire engine," you may introduce the third object: airplane. It is probably unwise to use more than three objects at a time with a young child, but when he can readily recognize the names of the ones you have been using, remove the ball and substitute a shoe. Later you may introduce other objects. Just be sure that they do not "look alike" on the lips.

As soon as he can recognize the names of a few objects, you can begin to vary the game. Let him watch while you "hide" three objects somewhere in the room. Then say, "Where is the ball? Get the ball." If he does not understand, lead him to the ball, and say, "There is the ball. Get the ball. Take it to the table. (Gesture with your eyes toward the table.) Put the ball in the box." Repeat the procedure with other objects.

You will be able to devise many activities of this sort. Remember, they must be enjoyed by the child. That means that they must be presented as "games" rather than "lessons in lip-reading." If he has difficulty in recognizing the name of one object, drop it before he becomes frustrated, and return to it later when he has acquired more skill. The ideal to strive for is the combination of enough "challenging difficulty" to keep the activity interesting, and yet see to it that the child meets with enough satisfying success to maintain his enthusiasm.

As you continue, he will learn that objects have names, and the chances are that he will begin to "ask" you to name objects for him just as a hearing child does—except that he will not use words to ask his question.

Later you may add to his vocabulary such words as "big" and "little" and the names of colors. For example, you present a "big ball" and a "little ball"; a "big fire engine" and a "little fire engine" in much the same way that you presented objects in your first game together. You may also present a "red ball" and a "yellow ball." Just be sure that the names of the colors you choose do not "look alike" on the lips.

Soon he will be ready for another vocabulary building activity —the construction of a scrapbook. On one page you may paste pictures of toys—not more than three to five on the page for they need to be well spaced. On another page you might have pictures of clothing, or foods, etc. The child may enjoy pointing to the pictures as you name them even more if he has had a hand in making the scrap book. The pictures may not be as neatly pasted, but who cares? We are more eager to develop and maintain his active interest than to prepare a "pretty book."

Since children will vary widely as to the age at which they are ready for various activities, and will also vary as to the rate at which they progress, it is impossible to advise you to "Start this activity at the age of 37 months and continue it for 5 weeks." This is where the personal conference is important. It should be pointed out that we are apt to do more harm than good if we begin these activities too soon or try to force the child to participate in them. On the other hand, there is no time to lose! Because the road to good communication for the deaf child is a long, rough trail, he should be started on it just as soon as he is ready, and helped to progress just as rapidly as he can happily go.

A knowledge of the characteristic interests and activities of hearing children at various age levels will be helpful. The advice (through correspondence or personal interview) of "experts" is desirable. In their absence, proceed with enthusiasm—but with caution.

help him learn to talk

Like the hearing child, the child who is deaf will learn to understand you before he begins to try to talk. You recall that in the normal development of speech, a child learns the meaning of many words before he begins to use any of them. This seems to be an essential part of the pattern, so the richer, more varied experiences you give him, the bigger the lip-reading vocabulary you help him acquire, the better the chances that he will learn to talk.

The first sounds that the infant makes are spontaneous—the result of air being expelled over the vocal folds that vibrate and create sound which is shaped or modified by the action of the lips and tongue. The baby who is deaf does this the same as the baby who hears. The hearing child then learns to imitate himself. This the deaf baby cannot do, for he cannot hear himself. However, the babbling sounds of the deaf baby are as sweet and pleasant as those that a hearing child makes. If we can keep him happy and relaxed as we encourage him to produce sounds, there is a better chance that his speech will have a pleasant, natural quality. If he is not encouraged to use his speech mechanism enough to keep it flexible, or if his efforts to produce sound are strained and tense, his voice is apt to become strained and unpleasant. It is important, then, to encourage him to produce sounds; whether or not the sounds resemble words is unimportant at this stage.

If, while you are holding the child and having him feel your cheek or throat, you gently move his hand to his own cheek or throat so that he can feel the vibrations as he vocalizes he may be encouraged to continue to make sounds. If he doesn't want to feel his own cheek, don't try to force the issue. Try it again tomorrow. When he is old enough, when he begins to sense some relationship between what he feels on your throat and what he feels on his own, and when he is sufficiently relaxed to enjoy quiet activities, but neither too excited nor too tired—when you catch just the right combination of all of these factors, you will be aware of a dawning interest on the child's part. But even when he shows an interest, don't try to prolong the session. His attention span is very short. Try it again later.

Before he is ready to start repeating words, it is a good idea to help him develop breath control. As a baby he practiced a quick inhalation followed by a prolonged exhalation when he cried. Now we want him to practice quick inhalation and prolonged exhalation for they are essential for speech. Blowing soap bubbles, blowing a feather or a ping-pong ball across a table, or blowing a boat or a duck in the bathtub—these and similar activities help him develop the breath control he will need for speech. Encourage these activities.

If, during the lip-reading "games" when you said "ball," he uttered a soft "aw" there's a cause for rejoicing. Try to understand what his sounds mean, and respond to them. A little quivering sensation in the throat may be the only awareness he has of the sounds that he makes. But if he finds that when he produces this sensation in his throat it brings about pleasant results, he has taken an important step toward learning to talk.

Often a mother begins helping her child to make speech sounds by holding the child on her lap in front of a mirror, so that he can watch her lips and his own. You will want to speak quietly and naturally. In teaching lip-reading you were urged to use simple sentences, but in teaching speech it is better to start with one syllable words. These words should be selected from those that have meaning for him because he can lip-read them. Encourage the child to imitate you. At first he may imitate only the movement of the lips, without making any sound. Hold his hand lightly against your cheek so that he can feel the vibrations, then against his own cheek as he tries to imitate you. If he produces a sound, show your approval. It may not sound like your word (or any word!), but reward him with your smile and encouragement.

Don't try for perfect articulation or pronunciation, and stop the activity as soon as the child tires of it. The work of improving pronunciation should be done by a teacher who is qualified by preparation and experience to tackle this complicated task. There will be many exercises and activities that you can do at home to supplement the work of the specialist, but they should be done only under the guidance or direction of the expert teacher.

Remember that the child will be more apt to develop an interest in acquiring speech if he discovers that it is useful. For that reason, be sure that the words you try to teach him are meaningful words, words that he can use. In your eagerness to have him talk, don't destroy the warm, comfortable relationship that you have with him. Too much pressure may do just that, and it isn't worth it. If you can make him aware of the flow of language and the rhythm of speech, you will have done a great deal. If you can encourage his production of sounds, that's excellent. But in most instances the help of a special teacher will be needed before he develops much intelligible speech. It's a slow process. It's harder on the child than it is on you. Since you can understand the problem, you will want to be patient and optimistic and helpful and patient.

Since a deaf child must see your face in order to "hear" or understand you, he may get the notion that you cannot hear him unless you are looking at him. This will be difficult to explain, but eventually he will understand. In the meantime, when he tries to communicate with you, you can help him avoid frustration and anxiety by looking at him. The very fact that you respond—even though you give him a drink when he asked for the ball—the very fact that you responded to his efforts at communication will encourage him to keep trying.

"You can lead a horse to water, but you can't make him drink," and you can lead a child to the table and go through all manner of drills, but you can't make him learn. As has been said before, he will learn best and most efficiently when he learns because he wants to know! So let's avoid long, dull drills. We will try to keep the lessons or games interesting—and this is more easily done when they are meaningful, when they are related to everyday experiences. Much of your teaching will occur during the fleeting moment when you have the child's attention in a situation that interests him. During the short time that the child is attentive, receptive, interested, give him as much as you can. But when he is tired or disinterested, it's time to stop.

Deaf children need to be alone now and then. They need to be away from the strain of trying to watch everything that is going on so as not to miss anything. You know how children who hear sometimes become over-stimulated so that they are cross and fussy; they are tired but they don't want to rest. The same thing can happen, perhaps more easily, to the deaf child. Try to arrange for him to have some quiet time when he can play as he wishes. He may play rather violently for a while—working off antagonisms as well as energy. But he needs some time for relaxed, free play.

These are some suggestions for helping your child along the road to communication and happy adjustment. They represent the best advice that I can offer. Of course, someone qualified in this field who knows you and your child could give more detailed suggestions and answer your questions more personally. Seek that help as soon as you can.

chapter x

some parting thoughts

CLASSROOM TEACHERS ARE usually interested in children and eager to do all that they can to help them. But their day is crowded. They have so many subjects to cover and so many children to teach that the amount of time that can be devoted to one child is necessarily limited. If a child stays with one teacher all day and she divides her time equally among her pupils, each child would receive about ten minutes of individual instruction per day. Most teachers do a remarkable job of "making time" for helping children who have special problems. Parents who stop to think of the pupil-time ratio are indeed grateful to the teacher who provides a little individualized help.

Parents are busy, too. Fathers must earn the living. Many mothers work, and most mothers have their hands full (especially if there are several children in the home) . But parents because they *are* parents have a special obligation to find the time that is needed for helping a child. A mother or father may skip a favorite radio or television program in order to give the child some extra time more easily than the classroom teacher can skip the reading or arithmetic lesson. It is possible for mother to wash the supper dishes or for father to read the paper after the child has gone to bed. No matter how busy parents are, they are clever enough to find time to help the child if they give a little thought to it.

With both parents and teachers, the problem is not so much "not being willing or able" as "not knowing what to do." This book has given you some ideas as to what can be done. The child's increased happiness, better adjustment, and improved communication will be sufficient reward for your efforts.

But of course the best intentions in the world do not take the place of the "know-how" that comes through study and experience. It is not too early to investigate the special education program of your school system. Do they conduct a hearing conservation program? Are speech correctionists employed? Are there special classes or other services for the children who need them? Most of the states provide a local school system with substantial financial assistance in conducting special education programs. Usually school authorities will do all that they can to provide "equal educational opportunities for all children" if parents point out the need. As members of a community, we cannot feel that we have met our obligation to all children until we have provided for the educational needs of those who need special help.

If you are contemplating a move to another community, in addition to housing facilities, employment possibilities, and the like, be sure to find out if the educational program includes the special help your child will need. If you cannot visit the community, write to the superintendent of schools. But avoid disappointment and frustration by finding out before you move if the educational needs of your child will be met.

In the meantime, the suggestions offered here will help you to do something constructive. But remember, this is a "first aid manual" and you should seek professional advice as soon as possible. Your child's future is in your hands.

INDEX